KIND·NESS
/'kīn(d)nəs/
DEFINED

by

OSEI DANIELS

Kindness Defined: Be kind, not nice. There is a difference.
Published by Watersprings Publishing,
a division of Watersprings Media House, LLC.
P.O. Box 1284 Olive Branch, MS 38654
www.waterspringsmedia.com
Contact publisher for bulk orders and permission requests.

Copyright © 2021 Osei Daniels. All rights reserved.

Editors: Maya Suero and Antoné Daniels

No part of this publication may be reproduced, distributed, or transmitted in any form or by any means, including photocopying, recording, or other electronic or mechanical methods, without the prior written permission of the publisher, except in the case of brief quotations embodied in critical reviews and certain other noncommercial uses permitted by copyright law.

Printed in the United States of America.

ISBN-13: 978-1-948877-88-6

Acknowledgements

To Karl and the Grounds Crew - You know who you are, It's OUR TIME NOW!

To the late Pastor Tony Mavrakos, He gave me the courage to be a maverick in ministry and not stay inside the frame—taking me across our country twice on a bike...changed my life forever. I will always REMEMBER.

To my late cousin, Wayne. Missing him even to this day...

My Brothers for Eternity: Michael, Brian, Tawanda, Thomas, Kojoe, Kevin, Cecil Jr, Aaron, Scott I, Sean, Phillip, Adedayo, Sheldon, and Ronnie Faminu (a.k.a. Fam, R.I.P)

Mentors: Pastor Diane Halverson, Mr. Cecil Calliste Sr., Joel Bullard Sr., Ps. Steve Murphy, Kwame Vanderhorst, Kymone Hinds and Dr. Myron Edmonds with the Men's Winning Circle.

To My Dad, Ronald Ellis Aubrey Daniels (R.E.A.D), MY Big Sisters: Malene, and Nneka (the Boss!), and the rest of the Daniels Family - We will move forward together, God is Able!

Our Bonus Daughter, Brittany...beautiful, smart, and a born leader, we believe in you!

To Antoné, my wife & ride or die! I understand what grace is every time I see that beautiful smile of yours. I love you more and more each day.

To my late mother, Daphne Emelda Daniels, who is to me and was indeed, KINDNESS DEFINED.

Praises for Kindness Defined

Merriam Webster defines communication as "the act or process of using words, sounds, signs or behaviors to express or exchange information or to express your ideas, thoughts, and feelings to someone else." Based on that description we can characterize communication as anything used to transfer a message from one person to another. Based on that, I firmly believe that the evolution of humanity is largely impacted by how we communicate. We can use the biblical account of the Tower of Babel as a case study. According to Genesis 11:6-7, "The Lord said, "If as one people speaking the same language, they have begun to do this, then nothing they plan to do will be impossible for them. Come, let us go down and confuse their language so they will not understand each other." In other words, just by altering the way we communicate our goals and desires as humankind can be thwarted.

Osei, in this book, takes us on a journey through his personal challenges, to help correct our understanding of the word kind. Over the last few decades, like many other words the definition of kind has been shifting and we no longer have a true and pure understanding of what it means. It doesn't mean being passive or agreeable, It doesn't mean simply reacting to life's circumstances. There is a deeper meaning that can lead us to freedom, confidence, and success!

- Karl Philips from Eric Thomas & Associates

Praises for Kindness Defined

"Who would have thought that being nice was so dangerous! Thankfully, Osei Daniels has helped to reprogram our psyche away from being nice to a revolution of being kind! Brilliant! Kindness has the power to reframing our existential experience in this world of being cancelled, shaded and feeling invisible if you don't get any likes on your social media post. An introspective reading of this work will help give you an edge in all your endeavors with people. What I appreciated most is that Daniels teaches us that kindness is not a disadvantage but rather the ultimate advantage to wherever you want to go in life. Read this book! All of it! And let's put kindness back in style."

- MyRon Edmonds, D.Min,
Winning Circle Leadership Group LLC

Table of Contents

Chapter 1: The Significant Differences between Being Nice and Being Kind 1
Chapter 2: My Story 9
Chapter 3: Life-changing Power of Kindness 17
Chapter 4: How to Become Kind 25
Chapter 5: How to be Kind to One's Self 35
Chapter 6: Professional Communication Skills 45
Chapter 7: Being Kind and Still Rising to the Top 59
Chapter 8: Kindness and Money 65
Chapter 9: Personal Communication Skills 73
Chapter 10: Relationships and Kindness 81
Chapter 11: Kindness in Uncomfortable Situations 91
Chapter 12: Kindness Towards Spouses and Significant Others 103
Chapter 13: Nice Guys DO Finish Last 117
Chapter 14: Communicating Displeasure 131
Chapter 15: A Channel of Blessing 135
Author Bio 139

Chapter 1
THE SIGNIFICANT DIFFERENCES BETWEEN BEING NICE AND BEING KIND

Nice, *adjective*
1 pleasing; agreeable; delightful:
2 amiably pleasant; kind:
3 characterized by, showing, or requiring great accuracy, precision, skill, tact, care, or delicacy

The word "nice" has been around for a long time and has multiple definitions. On the surface, being nice doesn't appear to be bad at all. I am okay with the word nice, but only when describing things and not people. For example, the small city of Nice, a port in and the capital of Alpes-Maritimes in Southeast France on the Mediterranean Sea is beautiful.

> Kindness is the ability to say NO with a smile.

Most people are primarily and culturally raised to be nice, and we have accepted the stature of being a nice person as the right, correct, and moral way to live. We describe various things as nice. The nice weather on a warm, not hot, summer day. We consider an outfit that is well put together and color-coordinated to be nice. Sports fans might cheer for a nice pass that results in a score. A violin might be labeled as nicely crafted, explaining the level of detail seen in the instrument. Countless other things are said to be "nice" in our everyday lives. But when it comes to describing the character of people, the word nice has absolutely no place!

Am I making a big deal out of nothing? My goal in this book is to make sure the word "nice" is never associated with one of us ever again! I believe it is outright dangerous regarding our overall character to be considered "nice." When the word nice is being used to describe a person, it gives me the feeling of hearing fingernails on a chalkboard. Nice should be used to describe things, never people. Instead, people should strive to be kind.

What is so bad about being nice? Unfortunately, being nice has led to the spread of the "nice guy/nice girl" disease, bringing tension and emotional illnesses to countless people. Three significant ways that being nice causes untold harm to ourselves and others.

1. Being agreeable leads to bitterness

My pastor taught me a life-changing principle. He said that "it is okay to disagree, but not okay to be disagreeable." I understood what he meant, having been part of various church board meetings for the majority of my adult life. I observed some board members find fault with every possible decision or direction that comes up during these meetings. These individuals have no obvious reasoning for disagreeing with the majority vote, seeming to speak negatively to be disagreeable.

Issues also arise with the opposite trait, when people are present in the meeting but are completely silent the whole time. This concept resonated with me deeply because I was the one who was always quiet. The challenge comes when someone who is quietly agreeable, someone who agrees at all times and who is never comfortable sharing their thoughts to the contrary, eventually becomes bitter.

Pain rises when someone harbors intense hostility. But what happens when these feelings are never expressed? Living with unexpressed bitterness will produce an emotionally toxic environment. It will cause a quiet, agreeable person to explode at the worst possible time, often towards the wrong people. Do you know anyone who always agrees with everything other people say, goes where everyone else wants to go, or does what everyone else wants to do? If so, you have a furious person on your hands, primed to explode.

2. Being coy or ingratiating is manipulative and will eventually be exposed

According to Dictionary.com, the word "ingratiate" means to establish in the favor or good graces of someone, especially by deliberate effort. Being ingratiating can potentially be manipulative and dishonest. The motives behind being ingratiating may get you what you want in the short term but will eventually be exposed for the lack of character it reveals.

Many of us have been around someone who initially comes off flattering. After a while, we get the feeling this person is attempting to get an angle on us. They speak incredibly modestly and smoothly. It pulls our guards down to the point where we believe almost anything they say. Those who are ingratiating invite us into particular decisions we would not make if we were truly aware of where they were coming from. Jesus says in John 3:20, "For everyone practicing evil hates the light and does not come to the light, lest his deeds should be exposed." The light here represents the truth. Those who are ingratiating do not want to be confronted and will hide behind "being nice." Instead, we will feel silly bringing up what we see as their underlying goal while facing their nice disposition.

3. Being perpetually shy can make us weaker as individuals and can lead to depression and low self-esteem

Growing up being painfully shy, I struggled with low self-esteem. I was always afraid, nervous, and walking on eggshells around people who I wanted to like me. I never felt comfortable in my skin. Though I had great friends, I could still see myself defaulting to being agreeable.

Like toggling between being in and out of shape physically, I believe everyone has emotional seasons of being agreeable as well. The challenge comes when we are continually living life while being shy. Depression will always be an arm's length away if we do not address this Now! It is time for the gifts, talents, and abilities that God has placed in us to be in full view!

Being confident in who we are while on our journey towards growth and maturity will give us the courage to speak up for ourselves and what we truly believe. Being constantly agreeable is like having an old operating system still running on your computer or smartphone. The upgraded system makes these devices faster and more efficient, and the same goes for us. We're going to look at how to install a character upgrade in our lives, which will make us the very best version of ourselves. What is this upgrade? Kindness!

Kind,
noun
the quality of being friendly, generous, and considerate.

adjective
1 of a good or benevolent nature or disposition, as a person
2 having, showing, or proceeding from benevolence
3 indulgent, considerate, or helpful; humane
4 mild, gentle, clement
5 loving; affectionate

The Bible's definition of kindness is from the Greek word, 'crestos,' which means serviceable, good, useful, pleasant. Here are some synonyms to help us define and frame the depth and breadth that kindness has:

> Good-natured, tenderhearted, warm, soft, good, caring, considerate, helpful, thoughtful, obliging, unselfish, selfless, altruistic, cooperative, magnanimous, friendly, amiable, gracious, public-spirited, tolerant, merciful, lavish, longsuffering, bountiful, philanthropic, handsome, princely

These are the definitions the dictionary and lexicons give us. I could spend a whole chapter defining these words and how they all point back to kindness. It is remarkable what kindness can do!

I don't think our society perceives the real difference between these two words. Nice and Kind. I believe with all my heart, in looking at both words at their best, that kindness will always trump being nice! Kindness is significantly more impactful to us personally, and those around us than being nice will ever be!

How many of us have seen people who are naturally benevolent ("desiring to help others, intended for benefits rather than profit")? This is a world where most people would step on the next person's neck if not for the consequences they would receive! We as a society often go to the complete opposite extreme of being nice. The antonyms of kindness are unkind, inconsiderate, mean, and cruel. We not only know these when we see them, but we also feel them. Sadly, some of us have dealt with these harsh realities for a long time.

The difference between kind and nice is subtle at first but stands out once you thoughtfully ponder the implications. With niceness, the person being nice and the person receiving the niceness can both do without it at any time. Say, for example, someone held the door for another person as they entered a store. This is nice and polite, but come on, how much extra effort and thought does this take? I mean, it is a "nice" thing to do, but if no one holds the door for us for the rest of the year, we will not be heartbroken. But when someone pays for your meal anonymously...something special happens! You will always remember the store, time of day, who was with you, and how inspired you were!

Kindness is deeply spiritual as well! Even with all the multiple versions of the Bible out there, none of them use the word nice. This is because the essence of what being nice means is not mentioned except in a negative connotation. However, kindness is mentioned all through the Bible! Being nice may be culturally accepted, but it is not life-changing!

I'll never forget when I was in junior high, my church youth group went on a trip. One of our youth leaders then, Keith Potts (one of my excellent youth leaders), was a caving expert. He wanted us to experience what he loved, so he brought extra carabiners, headlamps, helmets, and harnesses and took us somewhere deep in Virginia. None of us had ever done this before, so we were apprehensive, to say the least!

There we were about to do this (spelunking). As we got ready with the gear, he went on to prepare the way. We were all clipped onto a rope just in case any of us happened to slip on the wet rocks inside. We went in, following our fearless leader into a narrow, hard to maneuver, and pitch-black cave. As soon as all ten or so of us were inside, we were already wet, muddy, and cold.

We'd been spelunking for about twenty minutes and were about midway through the cave when he had everyone stop. We all had headlamps to be able to see our way, more or less, through one of the darkest environments I'd ever been in. He stopped and told everyone to turn off their headlamps. I was like, *"No way am I turning this light off!"* But after some convincing, we complied, and one by one, turned our lamps off. Let me tell you, I never thought I would ever *feel* darkness, but I felt it that day. I literally could not see my hand right in front of my face. It was unsettling, even though we only did it for like a minute. It was a minute that felt like an eternity. All of my senses felt attacked! Finally, he told us to turn the headlamps back on. I'd never been so thankful for light in my life!

I believe that our kindness will stand out like a flashlight in a dark cave during a spelunking adventure! Most of us have experienced kindness before and won't soon forget it. I am challenging each of you (and myself) to begin the journey toward kindness! I know our lives will be forever transformed as we shine a light on others. Let's GO!

Chapter 2
My Story

Hello, my name is Osei, and I was insecure. I struggled with insecurity for a significant portion of my life. While growing up, my family dynamic featured my mom, dad, and two older sisters. I was the baby of the family. We bounced between different apartments before finally settling in a house in the Northwest portion of the District of Columbia. Our home was small and quaint yet comfortable. Our neighborhood was calm, quiet, and safe, and it was situated on 5th Street, just a few blocks away from the Takoma Metro Station. Mom was a nurse, Dad was a teacher, and they worked very hard to afford where we lived.

> Treating others with kindness is the ultimate form of dignity.

My family was crucial for me growing up. We had a massive extended family, especially on my dad's side, where I had seven uncles and one aunt. On my mom's side, I had two uncles and one aunt. I vividly remember our family road trips up Interstate 95 to the Bronx and Brooklyn, New York, where my grandparents and the majority of my father's siblings lived. When we were not traveling, we would stay local with my mom's family in D.C.

Sadly, while growing up on 5th Street, one experience changed my life. When I was around ten years old, I was sexually molested by someone outside the family who happened to be staying with us for a while. This trauma severely stunted me and opened me up to the darkness of pornography. Already an introvert, the confusion and shame I felt caused me to isolate myself even further. Afraid to admit what had happened, I found myself lost in a world of illicit sexual images, magazines, and videos. Strangely, I believed what had happened to me was ok, but at the same time, I also knew I could never tell anyone what had happened. So, I kept it bottled up inside, having no idea what ramifications my silence would have on me for many years to come.

Growing up, I was intensely quiet and reserved, at least off of the basketball court. We were a low to a middle-class family, able to afford a home and car, but not many of the things I desired as a young boy, like name-brand shoes and clothes. I was always upset about going shopping and not being able to dress like the other students. My parents worked hard to be able to afford a Christian education for my oldest sister, Malene, and I. Nneka, my middle sister, has special needs, so she attended another school. I am genuinely grateful for the Adventist Christian education I received in elementary, middle, and high school. I would not be who I am today without it.

Making friends was one of the hardest things for me to do when we moved to Takoma Park, Washington DC. I was already painfully introverted when I got to my new school and the first couple of years were difficult for me. I was teased continuously for my dark skin and my lack of money. On top of that, not knowing anyone else was difficult for me. I was lonely, emotional, and completely unsure of myself. My only saving grace was basketball.

I was a lanky, dark-skinned adolescent who was always ready to go wherever my cousins wanted to go. During junior high, my cousins and I rode our big wheels (I know someone out there remembers when these were popular) up and down the street. Once we were old enough to ride bikes, there was no part of Northwest, DC we did not ride through. Aside from riding our bikes, we would also play ball at the Takoma Recreation Center. Riding around the city and playing basketball with them sparked my love for the sport.

Most of my weekends followed a similar pattern. I would go to my church on Saturdays (Sabbaths) and spend the night with my cousin Mortimer at my Uncle Wilfred and Aunt Connie's house. I would then go to their church with them on Sunday mornings, rush back home to change clothes, and then go straight to Hamilton court to spend the rest of the day playing ball until the streetlights came on.

This park had a popular basketball court where we would bring our own team: me, Mortimer, and a few of my other cousins, Mark, Greg, and Marlon. This court had the best basketball competition in the area (at least in my opinion). Still, with our dominating squad, we rarely lost a game, and it would be hard to get us off the court!

Many Sundays, we would play through the afternoon, but every once in a while, something special would happen. We would play a few games, and then abruptly, all the games on both of the two full courts would end. Cars would start to pull up around the court, and the elite ballers of the neighborhood would step out. Regardless of the score of the games we had been playing, these guys would put down their 40s (their alcohol) and blunts and take over the courts to immediately start their own game. To me, it was the best basketball I had ever seen live! People from all over seemed to come and stand around the court's perimeter to watch these guys dribble, pass and shoot a thousand times better than what I had been admiring on television.

As I matured, I pieced together the reason these guys only played at Hamilton court and not professionally. They arrived at the park drunk and high, and left continuing the same habits. I felt sad everyone did not get to see these guys on TV, but in my heart, I knew they would never get there while doing what they were doing. Regardless, watching these guys play at such an elite level increased my love for basketball, which I played with passion.

I was tall and played with tons of energy, so I earned a spot on the junior high basketball team at John Nevins Andrews School. Brad Durby, one of the most influential people in my life, was my coach. Coach Durby believed in me and gave me a chance to flourish. The older I got, the better I got, building confidence in my skills every day.

I will never forget how loud it got during the home games in our tiny school gym! The crowd, cheerleaders, and teammates would get me and everyone excited. By my eighth-grade year, I began getting a lot of attention for my basketball skills. Parents and even high school kids started coming to watch me play. We had such a great squad with Matt, Rajesh, Phillip, Bill, Milfred, and others. Man, those were great days!

Though I was a star in middle school on the basketball court, off the court was a completely different story! I still had zero confidence in myself. I liked girls but would NEVER have enough courage to go and talk to any of them. The one "relationship" I did have in middle school at the time only lasted one day. Yup...just one day. My friends, knowing how shy I was, pretty much forced it upon both of us. I barely even had time to tell anyone I had a girlfriend when, the next day, my friend told me it was indeed over. There was no kiss, not even a hug. I was both devastated and humiliated.

When I moved to high school, I had some clout for my basketball skills. My middle school coach even came with us and began teaching and coaching at Takoma Academy as well. Being overly confident in my game, I told myself, "*Oh, I'm a shoo-in to make the team, no need to practice or get better!*" When the team list came out after try-outs, to my and my friend's shock, I did not make the team. This disappointment was yet another devastating blow to my already fragile self-esteem. Through this disappointment, I became more determined than ever to make the team the next year, and I did. I played for the rest of high school on the varsity team. I was even offered a partial scholarship to play college basketball at a school in Massachusetts.

But, because the school did not have a huge budget at the time, I chose not to take the offer. I wanted to avoid complicating things for my mom and dad (another example of me being too nice). I was blessed that my mom was a nurse at Howard University Hospital, which enabled me to attend Howard University for free. If I am honest though, I wish I had given it at least one year to challenge myself and play college ball. Instead, I chose the path of least resistance.

While at Howard, I never had a girlfriend. I will always remember the time during my freshman year when I was captivated by a young lady. After some time of mustering up the courage, I finally asked her out. She agreed, and we went to see the University of Maryland Gospel Choir Concert—my first official date. Unfortunately, I found out the hard way that some girls can be as mean and manipulative as some guys can. To sum up the situation, the next time I asked her out, she wanted to bring her friend and have me pay for everything for both of them. Even though I was lonely and desperately wanted a girlfriend, I knew I should not put up with being taken advantage of in this manner.

Beginning my sophomore year, I continued to be heavily involved in activities at my church. Growing up, I was part of Pathfinders (the Adventist version of Boy Scouts), and Keystone, our youth group. During my time in Keystone, my youth leader Phil Sing gave me such guidance and encouragement when I needed it. He was the edgy, in-your-face leader who showed us that no topic was taboo. He was a crisis counselor for a group home, and he would tell us stories of all the issues and drama that his teens and young adults were involved in there. It was intense and sometimes shocking but motivating as well.

Consequently, it was nothing for me to continue going to Keystone, help out in random church events, and go to feed the homeless every week. Throughout high school and college, my friends and I loved making sandwiches and going downtown every week to hand them out with Mr. Calliste. Aaron, Scott, Sean, and I would even make weekly runs to pick up the food we would need to pack up and feed the homeless. I eventually became known as Mr. Dependable: always trustworthy, available, and willing to help.

At one point, I even became the youth group "taxi cab." This led to countless late-night expeditions after our youth group programs, retreats, and other social activities. As youth leaders, Aaron, Scott, Sean, and I would drive all over D.C. and Maryland, dropping teens off at home. Most of the youth who came to our events had no other way of getting back home. We had the keys to the church van, so we drove them all around the DMV and loved it! Over time, I eventually became the church janitor, security guard, occasional youth speaker, youth trip coordinator, actor in church plays, Bible worker, and soundboard technician amid other roles.

Aside from participating, I even shifted into leadership roles. I became the leader of the Adventist Fellowship group on campus at Howard University, the youth elder at Takoma Park Church, and eventually the youth director. I was ALWAYS at church and helping with everything as I still struggled with saying no. But with all of this, no one knew all the frustration I had in my heart, not even me.

My frustration silently boiled over and eventually turned into intense bitterness. I began to hate church, not wanting to go at all. But, because I knew people depended on me, I ignored my feelings and went regardless. I realize now that all I did back then was an attempt to avoid thinking about the sexual trauma I experienced right before entering junior high. With this lingering trauma, combined with my unresolved insecurity and lack of self-confidence, the result was I simply could not say no. I felt pressure and guilt in wanting to serve God and the church, and I did not want to let my pastor, elders, and other church leaders down. I learned early on how to pretend and smile. Always showing up to the church and helping out were all attempts to hide what I was wrestling with on the inside.

When I graduated from Howard after a five-and-a-half-year grind, something happened to me that changed EVERYTHING. I attended a weekend seminar at my church called "Binding the Wounds," facilitated by Ron and Nancy Rockey. I had never heard about actual freedom from past abuse and trauma before then! I decided that I did not want to be bound to pornography anymore, and I wanted to be free from my insecurities and low self-esteem. I knew this weekend event was something I desperately needed.

Through attending the seminar and the help of their book, *Belonging*, I was finally on the road to freedom! As I directly faced past issues, I became more confident, less afraid, and more willing to continue my journey towards healing and purity. Since then, I have been blessed to have found the love of my life, Antoné, and we now serve faithfully at our church. I even served as a Youth Pastor for five years—this time, by choice and not through guilt or insecurity.

I am eternally grateful for my journey thus far in life! My life changed when I stopped running and hiding behind being nice. I found out for myself that kindness can lead to freedom, confidence, and success! I'm excited to now share those life-changing thought patterns with you.

Chapter 3
LIFE-CHANGING POWER OF KINDNESS

Kindness has the life-changing power to transform you from the inside out. It will impact your health, confidence, your view of yourself and others, and the world around you. Buckle up and get ready to have your life transformed through the power of kindness!

One of the most challenging times of my life happened after leaving Howard University. I graduated with an engineering degree in computer science right when the dot.com industry boom slid from underneath my fledgling career. I did get job offers before I graduated, but between listening to my pride and misinformed classmates, I balked at their low salary offers.

> Kindness: you know it when you see it.

I went through countless job site searches, interviews, and a few short-term contracts, which didn't amount to anything significant. I grew desperate enough to head down to the unemployment office in D.C., but they did not have anything for me either. I had a few part-time jobs during this time before I finally got a position as the custodian at the General Conference Office for the Seventh Day Adventist Church, where the majority of my time was spent in the basement shredding papers.

I remember, at one point during this period, I got into a heated argument with my mom where I raised my voice and slammed the door (which I never did) because she felt like I was not trying hard enough. Then, one day, I went to church asking for prayer to get a full-time job. A fellow church member, feeling sympathy for me, shook my hand and said she would be praying for me. I thanked her and was on my way out to my car when I glanced down and noticed something in my hand. When I opened my hand, I found a folded $20 bill inside of it... I had never felt so utterly empty in my life. I felt like a complete failure! Though physically standing 6 feet 4 inches high, my humiliation and discouragement made me feel like I was only 2 inches tall. But God!

Because I was willing to be honest about my struggles while looking for employment, an unexpected door opened. A kind-hearted teacher, Ms. Nina Huff, found out I was looking for a job. She told me there was an opening at her elementary school as the Computer Lab Instructor. I thought to myself, *"I don't want to teach!"* but I decided anything was better than shredding papers, so I decided to go in for the interview. I blinked, and I have now spent 17 years employed with the school system. God is ABLE! Soon after I began working, I was able to afford my first condo, and I was finally ready to leave my parents' basement.

I wasted a lot of time with online dating during those early days of independence, and I had just about given up on ever finding someone special. A few years later, I found the love of my life on Yahoo Personals (I know, we're old), and I have had 14 years of marriage bliss ever since! Ms. Huff's kindness opened the door for me to step into the next season in my life. I am not sure where I would be today without her humbling display of consideration towards me.

In my personal life, kindness has opened doors for me, which otherwise were shut tight. I now have a deep desire to help propel the kindness movement by showing kindness to others. Here are some significant benefits our kindness can have for us and others.

1. Kindness creates space for more joy in our hearts

If we look at our heart like a typical closet, there is a limited amount of stuff it can hold. Instead of clothes, our hearts are full of emotional and spiritual stuff, which cannot be counted, touched, or moved physically. We all need to ask ourselves; what kind of things are currently in our hearts? The majority of us are clueless about what we are holding onto.

Life has a way of revealing all that is hidden inside, regardless of how deep we stuff things into the back of our closets. Each one of us must take time in our lives to regularly do some much-needed introspection. How much fear, anger, jealousy, and bitterness are we holding inside our hearts? Do we even know? Are there more positive than negative things in there? We need to know what we're holding because what is in our hearts usually determines our decisions and how we feel about ourselves, others, and the world around us. When we choose to hold onto negative thoughts, patterns, mindsets, disappointments, and anger, then we simply do not have space in our hearts for kindness.

God has the utmost respect for us. Even though He knows we will make poor choices over and over again, He will not take anything from our thoughts and minds without our expressed permission. In order to remove the harmful feelings in our hearts, we must recognize and admit that they are harmful. Then we must declare to God that we acknowledge these are not helping us whatsoever and give Him permission to prune these things out of our hearts. Why do we have to give permission to God? I've heard it said that God is a gentleman, and He will not force us to do what we do not want Him to do. Look at 1 John 1:9, "If we confess our sins, He is faithful and just to forgive us our sins and to cleanse us of all unrighteousness." The word "if" here is crucial! Here is the order: The Holy Spirit reveals to us all the unrighteous things in our hearts, we confess them to God, and He does the cleansing.

Once we have removed these harmful items from our hearts, we now have room for joy. The Greek word for joy is *chara*, which means delight and gladness. It is one of the fruits of the Spirit, found in Galatians 5. Joy is not happiness. Happiness refers to "a state of feeling or showing pleasure or contentment." Joy, which we see mentioned throughout the Bible, is a sustained place, not a transitory state that tends to change on a dime.

Jesus confidently said before He would be crucified in John 16:22, "So you have sorrow now, but I will see you again; then you will rejoice, and no one can rob you of that joy." This is the joy we can experience in our hearts once we remove all the hidden obstacles. This joy is unexplainable to people who do not have a consistent connection to Jesus. We can experience the worst that life has to throw at us and have sustained joy, confidently knowing that Jesus will be with us in the storm and help us make it through with a smile!

2. Kindness rebuilds broken bridges

We have all made bad choices in our lives. Many of those bad decisions have caused issues in our relationships. Some minor, some major. Our negative and emotional issues can weaken the bridge of communication between our loved ones and us, leaving us unsure how to rebuild it. Some of us will simply ignore the other person, acting as if nothing happened, and others of us are too prideful to admit our fault in the situation. Either way, this is not the end.

To repair physical bridges, construction engineers perform a process called retrofitting. Retrofitting involves adding a new component or accessory to the structure that was not there when the bridge was originally manufactured. This process can not only repair the current damage but prevent future damage from being catastrophic in the case of a major ground-shaking event. Kindness is the retrofit that our damaged relationships need. Kindness brings damaged feelings to the surface. Kindness doesn't pretend that nothing is wrong but courageously opts for uncomfortable conversations. It has a desire only for the good of the relationship, not to save the pride of either person.

One person in an altercation may act more maturely than the other and be willing to reach out first. We can quickly get stuck on the details of who made the first move, but this only serves to delay the reconnection as the goal is restoration. Kindness calls on the more mature person to make the first move, even knowing there is a chance that the other person will not understand, agree, or even be willing to connect again. I also challenge those who believe what the Bible says to test its guidance where the person who has received the offense should go to the offender and be willing to forgive and work things out with them. With kindness, the process can begin to create the construction zone for the relationship to begin building again.

3. Kindness expands our influence

In our world of bad news being pumped at us 24/7 through the media, we could use a boost from time to time. Kindness produces power! It has a way of changing the atmosphere of a room, a bad day, or a sad moment instantly. Choosing ourselves to be a part of that change takes our attitude to such a refreshing level. We might say, "I wish I had always been doing this!" There is an addictive aspect of kindness that has zero negative consequences. When we choose to be kind, we are satisfied, and we want more!

Kindness has a unique power to build influence. Jesus was teaching the Samaritan woman at the well when He said, "Whoever drinks of this water will thirst again, but whoever drinks of the water that I shall give him will become in him a fountain of water springing up into everlasting life!" John 4:13-14. One of the most incredible stories of Jesus' life was His interaction with this woman at the well. Jesus showed this woman kindness when she deliberately went to the well at a time when she knew no one else would be there to judge or criticize her. He cared about her soul! This one woman, with numerous challenges, ended up leading an entire town to the Kingdom of God!

Do we care for others? I mean, genuinely care, without any ulterior motives? Are we kind just for the sake of being kind? Are we willing to do for and ask things of others that most will not? If we are, our impact is about to blow up! After one conversation with Jesus, this woman completely forgot the reason she came to the well at all, leaving behind her condemnation, her self-loathing, and her shame, and went to share the Water of Life with everyone in her town!

Let's pause for a second. I hear your brain working, saying, "Ok, of course, Jesus could do that! But I do not have the water of life! There is no way one conversation with me will motivate people enough to change anything they are currently doing." I hear you, but I disagree.

Isaiah 55:11 states, "So shall my word be that proceeds out of my mouth; It shall not return to me void, but it shall accomplish that which I please, and it shall prosper in the thing for which I sent it." This is a spiritual principle that God Himself is responsible for the results of His Word. He has the power to make our kindness yield a harvest that He knows whoever we are interacting with needs. The REAL challenge is finding who will choose to be His willing vessel? Will you?

Our acts of kindness have a significant influence on others, but many times it takes a while for the seed to begin to grow! I believe we as Christians are "seed planters," spreading acts of kindness around in such abundance in our daily lives and praying that each one will produce a harvest. It is humbling when sometimes we are blessed to see the results instantly, but the majority of the time, we do not.

But does it mean we stop planting? A thousand times NO! I believe the woman at the well was so excited to share her newfound joy that she did not even care if people understood what she was saying. The kindness shown to her was so genuine and pure. This kindness was what she needed to turn her life around.

Many times, being kind requires us to have tough conversations with others. But kindness—the kind smile or look, or the willingness to stay late, arrive early, and even maybe give up a parking spot—might be just what it takes. We'll be so stoked by merely making the kind gesture that we can move on, trusting the process will produce what God has planned for it to do. God just needs somebody to be KIND!

Chapter 4
How to Become Kind

Treating ourselves kindly is essential. The Bible tells us 11 times that we are to love our neighbor as ourselves. We understand how we are to love our neighbor, but we bypass the instruction to love ourselves. As a result, many are stuck in a form of pseudo-righteousness, where they believe that doing more for others will make them look better in God's eyes. Not only is this not biblical, but it brings us dangerously close to pride, which God hates. Proverbs 16:18 says, "Pride goeth before destruction, and a haughty spirit before a fall."

> You cannot give what you do not have.

So, what does treating ourselves kindly look like? How do we replace the playlist stuck on repeat that says, "I am selfish if I put myself first"? Many of our minds flood with thoughts of negativity and self-defeat, such as, "How could you be so stupid!?" or "Only a loser would have made that mistake!" or "You are a failure!"

I struggled with these thoughts myself. Then I read a book called *The Power of Prayer* by Roger Morneau. Morneau said that the devil when he is tempting us can whisper to us, in our own voice. He might say something like, "I want to eat this third piece of the pie," when he knows our weaknesses are sweets. Whether or not you believe the source, these thoughts are still on repeat in our heads.

Our minds are powerful. How we feel about ourselves determines our thoughts, and our thoughts then determine our actions. We have to find tangible ways to avoid destructive patterns and learn healthy methods to deal with challenging situations while treating ourselves kindly in the process.

Sadly, a large percentage of us have never been taught how to be kind to ourselves. The time for this re-education must begin today! If we cannot give what we do not have, what are we offering? We are giving away our margin. Our margin is the mental, emotional, and spiritual space that separates us from others. As the margin becomes thinner and thinner, so does our ability to prevent harmful aspects of our lives from occurring. Depression, frustration, and hurt feelings will manifest themselves in our lives if we do not become kind to ourselves. Here are ways for each of us to become kind to ourselves.

1. Choose to be kind

Every day we have choices to make. Options like when to wake up, what to eat, what to wear, which path to take to work, whether to attend class, what to spend money on. Our choices go beyond our general routine to questions like, what will be our focus for the day? What will our attitude be towards work, class, home, spouse, children, friends, and strangers? Some choices are harder than others to make and to make consistently.

Our lives can go by so quickly that it feels like we can barely even think; better yet, be deliberate in the choices we make. I tell my young people all the time, "You will never have time for everything, but you will have time for your priorities." What are our priorities? Another saying I repeat to the youth is meant to help them identify their priorities and thus determine what choices they'll make. I remind them, "To say no, you have to have a bigger yes." Our job is to find our "Bigger Yes" and to keep that goal in mind as we make decisions.

Being kind is a choice. We first have to decide and then make it a habit. Phillippa Lally, a European health psychology researcher at University College London, published a study in 2009 showing it takes up to 66 days to form a new habit. Some may say they are simply too busy to begin building any new habits, much less work on a habit of being kind. Others are stuck in the immature thought pattern of treating others how they treat us.

Choosing to be kind takes courage! We stand out when we deliberately choose not to mirror how we are treated and treat others the way we want to be treated. That choice includes moments of conflict. Some might look forward to arguments or disagreements, but many nice people are simply afraid of conflict. Being kind does not erase conflicts. There will be conflicts, but it means how we respond to them will keep our hearts free and clear of unspoken issues, disagreements, and potential resentment. So that regardless of what kind of treatment we get, we choose not to give the same. We can take the offensive posture and be confident in who we are as Christians! We do not need to be overly aggressive, but we can be bold where we stand and speak kindly towards others' perspectives.

Taking the offensive posture pushes us to strive to be the very best version of ourselves every day so that we can give God the best possible shine. Simply put, Christians are to be peacemakers, not by avoiding conflicts or uncomfortable situations, but by being the solution to problems in today's world, exactly where we are placed.

2. Learn to be comfortable with people not understanding

Kindness is rarely seen, and because it is so rare, it will be easily misunderstood. It is so abnormal that it will stand out like a really tall person in a crowd. I believe many are apprehensive about being kind to others because it will draw attention from those around us. Being nice is what is normally acceptable and overall pleasant and attractive to everyone, but kindness is all about function! It is helping in a specific way that was not expected. It is about being sensitive to a need and willing to address it, strictly based on our ability to do so. Being nice is like car wax. Our car will look great, but it won't get us anywhere! Kindness is like gas for our car.

Kindness is important! The key again is not going overboard but trusting that God will give us plenty of opportunities to bless and serve others that match our gift and ability to do so. We need to be prayerfully willing to make our divine appointment for that day and time. We, as Christians, must learn to be comfortable in this space! We have to believe that God is deliberate where and when He has placed His "Tools" to be used to bless others!

3. Unlearn unhealthy habits and thought patterns

We have habits and tendencies that we need to unlearn and remove from our minds and hearts so God can replace them with His principles! We see in the book of Luke that we can't just remove the negative habits without replacing them with something positive. Until we make a choice to allow God to remove them and replace them, we will never truly be kind.

A lot of times, we only focus on what we should be avoiding in life. What not to do, what not to say, where not to go. But what about what we *should* do, say, and think? We hear a lot of don'ts, especially in the church, which pushes many, especially young people, to think of God, the Bible, and Christianity only in restrictive terms. That's a shame. Our goal is to change the negative, sinful paradigm of righteousness by works to obedience from love and appreciation.

New, better thought patterns come into our lives by consciously forming a habit. We have to consistently implement tactics that will help us to not only remove the habits we no longer want in our lives but give us something better and more sustainable in their place. Like, when we want to eat some sugary dessert, we can prepare ahead of time for when that thought comes up. We can have a better alternative ready, like pineapples, grapes, oranges, cantaloupe, or watermelon. Along with planning, we need knowledge about our specific struggles so we can have a plan of attack to counter the thoughts that tend to arise in our minds. We need to start showing kindness to ourselves so that we can be available to show kindness to others!

4. Form strong yet flexible limits

An excellent resource for adults to learn to set appropriate limits is the book Boundaries by Dr. Henry Cloud. We find an explanation in the Bible as well. Galatians 6:2 says, "Bear ye one another burdens, and so fulfill the law of Christ." And verse 5 says, "For every man shall bear his own load." These two verses break down the principle of what forming healthy boundaries includes. Simply put, we are responsible TO others (verse 2) but FOR ourselves (verse 5).

There are certain things that everyone alive (pending mental and physical challenges) should be able to do for themselves and take responsibility for. Verse 2 says that we are to "carry each other's burdens." The Greek word for "burden" is *baros*, which literally translates to a massive boulder, a rock so heavy that it would be impossible for one person to carry alone for any great distance. These boulders represent trauma, abuse, addictions, and physical and emotional injuries that must be addressed with the help of others. We should be willing to help as part of small groups and one-on-one and turn to others for support when we need it. This is a way of showing the kindness that I believe God has called us to engage in.

But some things are for us to do for ourselves, as we see in verse 5. The word "load," *phortion* in Greek, is like a knapsack that can be carried around daily by one person alone. Every child needs to learn to be responsible for themselves at some point. I have seen the lack of responsibility play out in our society. I see young ladies doing big things like getting scholarships and finding great jobs, but I see our young men are coddled and mothered to death. They have no aspirations, no goals, and no desires in them, for the most part. Many spend their days smoking weed, playing video games, and getting girls pregnant. Children need capable examples of adult men and women to help guide and encourage them. We have to lovingly and kindly tell our children that they are more than capable of doing certain things for themselves. We have to teach and empower them, giving them space to make bad choices while still at home. Then they'll be able to go out into the world with lessons learned and confidence built that they could take great care of themselves and make informed decisions for their lives and futures.

A lot of the issues and challenges surface when we confuse the two roles of being responsible to others and for ourselves. What would the life of the church look like if we were to lovingly and kindly hold people accountable in this way? We would be more durable, wiser, and have more of a positive influence on our society. Our communities would notice and want in on the secret. Choosing to be kind is difficult initially (like going to the gym after a while), but when we consistently work through the pain and soreness, we build endurance and strength in expanded areas. The same will happen when we put in the work of choosing to be kind.

5. Practice forgiveness

No one finds it easy to forgive others. Just the idea of it can drive many of us crazy. Whether someone hurts us accidentally or deliberately, we're still faced with the choice of whether to forgive them or hold them in contempt.

I will never forget during my freshman year at Howard University when I lost my wallet. At least I thought I lost it. While playing basketball at the university's gym, I put my stuff next to some guys who were waiting on the sidelines. It's embarrassing how naive I was then. I finished playing and went to get my things, only to find that my wallet was gone. I went around asking some of the guys if they'd seen it, and one guy actually helped me look for it. As we were searching, he started asking questions that made me a little uncomfortable, including specific personal details that he clearly did not need to know. At one point, he even asked something about my social security number. I just played it off and did not give it to him. I had seen him at the gym many times, so I didn't think much of it. We didn't find my wallet that night, so I had to go through all the annoying hoops of canceling my bank cards and getting a new license.

A few weeks passed, and I got a replacement license, bank card, and school ID. I had mostly forgotten about the whole thing until I found out that someone was trying to use my information. Someone had gone to a local bank to try to open up a new account in my name. Only by God's grace, the person at the desk was suspicious of the man trying to do all of this, and when she saw the license he attempted to use, she knew right away that he was a criminal. The teller told the man that because the license was not his, he could not open an account. The thief said, "Oh ok, cool. No problem," and then he walked out of the bank. I know God is real and that He is looking out for me because the bank teller he was trying to lie to was my cousin, Noelle! If He had gone anywhere else, he might have been successful. But thankfully, I was able to learn the details of what happened, and I even got my original license back.

After this incident, I saw the same guy on campus again. Being the nice guy that I was at the time, I played it off like I did not know what he had done. I asked him if he'd ever happened to come across my wallet since the day he helped me search for it. He made up some lie, and, after that, I never saw him again. I've wondered about what someone else might have done in that situation. Call campus police and report him? Go to him outright and tell him that they knew what he did? Deep down, I did not have it in me to confront him in this way. But, I will say, when criminal activity is involved, we should always contact law enforcement. We must be smart and not try to be a hero!

Part of my issue with confrontation stemmed from my childhood when I was sexually molested. It was the weirdest, most uncomfortable, and most confusing situation that I had ever experienced. I knew it was wrong but simply did not have the voice to say it and try to get myself away from the situation. No one else, except one person, ever knew what happened, and I bottled up all these emotions for years. To grow comfortable with confrontation, I had to address the issues I still struggled with from my childhood.

I share all of this to encourage you that yes, harmful, hurtful things may have happened to us, but we can forgive and move on from them. But the key to this process is that, just because you forgive someone, it does NOT mean that you make yourself vulnerable to their abuse, attack, or presence again! Dr. Cloud's book, Boundaries highlights this point.

I had to do my work. I had to be willing to go back to that situation and confess my thoughts and feelings about them in a safe space and allow God to remove the painful emotions connected to the experience. For so long, each time it came to mind, or I faced a similar situation of theft or abuse, however slight, my heart would flood with the same hurt and take me back to that initial experience over and over again. I had to choose to no longer allow these experiences to direct my life, my thoughts, and my decisions. It was by God's grace that I started my journey toward healing at Ron and Nancy Rockey's small group, "Binding the Wounds." I learned to forgive the people who hurt me and forgive myself for what I had done in response to that pain.

Forgiving yourself can be one of the most challenging things a human being has to do. We focus our existence on doing "good" things to earn positive rewards and on being penalized for the wrong things we do. We have prisons and corporal punishment for offenders and lesser penalties for minor offenders. Our system doesn't do well at welcoming these individuals back into the community after paying their debts to society.

Almost as bad as our prison system are the personal prisons we hold ourselves in for years, and sometimes for the majority of our lives. We leave ourselves in these mental, emotional, and spiritual prisons, locked in shame and guilt. Again, making part of our salvation what we do instead of who we know.

Many have not yet experienced the fact that God can heal and free us all from the traumatic experiences we have had and that we can avoid enduring similar hurt again. I believe the church needs to do a better job of empowering our members with this truth! Spirit-filled Christian counselors and therapists can help you throughout this process. Spiritual issues do not expire or disappear on their own. We have to address them in order to heal from them. This, to me, is the Gospel of Jesus Christ! The Gospel gives us freedom from the penalty, power, and presence of sin!

There is forgiveness that only Jesus Christ can give us. When we accept His forgiveness, we know that we will never be able to pay back our debts to God and that He does not expect us to! What an awesome exchange! Because we have been forgiven by God, accepting His forgiveness allows us to be willing to forgive others, which is one of the kindest things we can ever do!

Chapter 5
HOW TO BE KIND TO ONE'S SELF

Our self-care must become our priority! Dictionary.com defines self-care as "care for self without medical or other professional consultation." This phrase is becoming increasingly relevant due to our society's focus on obtaining life balance. The bottom line is, we can only give so much before replenishing ourselves so that we can do more. Taking care of our physical health, mental stability, and spiritual direction can truly be accomplished by ourselves or amongst a group of like-minded people without having to depend on professionals or waiting for something to go wrong with us. The key is to be proactive with the limits we set for ourselves with others.

> We cannot give to others what we do not already possess.

So many people do not take great care of themselves. I am a big proponent of self-care because it is the ultimate form of kindness to ourselves. Let me explain. There is a warped version of the Christian faith. Somehow there is a belief that in giving everyone absolutely everything we have, including our time, resources, and emotional energy, we are 'serving' God. Many believe this is wise, healthy, and even biblical. Even though the Word of God clearly states in Galatians 5:14 that we are to "love our neighbor AS OURSELVES." We, in the church, have overlooked this vital aspect of the verse more times than not. Plainly stated: We cannot give what we do not have.

This twisted view also exists outside the church. Sadly, many of us get our worth and value from doing things for everyone else. We strain ourselves so much that we lose our overall health and other critical personal resources. When we do not take care of ourselves we then put tons of pressure on our families, friends, and those in our communities to help 'fix' us. I want to empower both those inside and outside the church to recognize the importance of self-care. Once we really love ourselves by prioritizing our self-care, we place ourselves in a better position to help others. We must first show love to ourselves and THEN to others.

So far, we have created an unhealthy precedent to avoid the look of prioritizing care for ourselves, so that we will not appear selfish. This same rationale makes church work and church attendance the priority, while self-care, family time, and our health trail behind. Self-care pushes us to prioritize our mental, emotional, physical, and spiritual well-being so that we can give our very best to God and those He wants us to help. Self-care is the definition of kindness! How can we help others the way God wants us to if we have not grown, matured, and equipped ourselves properly first? Even as I write this, this antiquated paradigm rings as 'selfish' in my mind. I have made myself a victim of church work and attendance many times to feel acceptable to God. Our church and its leaders have shown themselves 'faithful' to God, but sadly our health and connection to our families have suffered greatly. Kindness will help us to reprioritize our time and effort to be God's best.

There are five practical and immediately applicable benefits of self-care in light of the ultimate goal of kindness. Self-care provides us with a sense of renewal, produces 'GOD-fidence,' makes kindness contagious, prevents anxiety and depression, and increases our social awareness. Kindness has a treasure-trove of benefits that will make life more exciting to live and experience. Let's get into it!

1. Sense of renewal

Work, in and of itself, can be very exhausting! We must prioritize self-care weekly to be effective in the long term. At Creation, God set up the Sabbath for us to enjoy at the end of each week. The Sabbath is a beautiful reminder of God's creative and restorative power in the world and our lives individually. Just as our blood cells reproduce themselves every day, our brain cells need to do the same. Each week, we need an opportunity to disconnect from all our work responsibilities to recalibrate and give our minds a break. Science has proven that people who participate in a weekly sabbath, where they focus on rest and rejuvenation and do not work, are much healthier than those who don't. This day of rest helps us to return to work with a clear head to focus on the tasks of the upcoming week.

I have no idea how people can go years and years of never giving themselves time to pause, rest, and think of things other than work. I get the idea of grinding to accomplish goals for yourself financially, but what happens when we achieve our goals, but our health is woefully inadequate, and our close relationships are severed? The money will not be able to repair the loss experienced here. Time to breathe, rest, think, process, help others, pray, study the Bible, visit with friends and family, and worship can all occur on the Sabbath!

My wife and I believe the Bible calls this day Saturday. There is NOTHING better than looking forward to more than being together as a couple with like-minded believers on Sabbaths. Some weeks, we spend the day at home together to talk, reflect, share our visions, and hang out with friends and family. I encourage you to prioritize your overall health and make the Sabbath a part of your weekly routine. It will be the kindest thing you have ever done for yourself!

2. Self-care produces 'GOD-fidence'

I believe a big reason many people struggle personally and emotionally is a poor sense of self. The Christian community has placed an extremely high value on putting others first and serving others, and I agree that serving others is important. The question is, what happens to us individually if we are always giving of ourselves to allow others to receive? I have heard and agree that we cannot give what we do not have. If we do not make it a priority to make time for ourselves to gain a sense of renewal from the Sabbath, self-care, and quality time with loved ones, we can never give others our best, much less give it to God! God needs us to operate at our optimal level so we can accomplish His will through our lives in our homes, jobs, communities, and the world. But I know from personal experience when we always give to others without taking proper care of our physical, emotional, mental, and spiritual health, that we are at significant risk of harboring feelings of bitterness, frustration, and disappointment.

A lot of times, many of us are helpful to a fault. We are always saying yes, seeking to be Mr. or Ms. Dependable, and secretly taking pride in it. We enjoy having everyone else think we are the ones they can count on to get things done. But I want us to consider something. If we are always there to do what is needed, we not only burn the candle at both ends, but we block others from having the opportunity to help and grow themselves. We take so much pride in being dependable! Being dependable is a strong character trait and should be admired, but the question is, how far is too far? If we do not show up for every single event, program, call, job, or meeting, what is the worst thing that could happen? And if we're honest, we could use a break.

We need time to gain a sense of identity, to be refreshed, to learn more about ourselves, to connect more closely to God and our family, and sometimes to just be still. But we choose not to. Why? One of my favorite quotes from C.S. Lewis says, "True humility is not thinking less of yourself; it is thinking of yourself less." We all need a sense of renewal, which comes with true humility, but not at the cost of individual significance.

Humility is not the same as humiliation. According to Dictionary.com, humility means "to have a modest opinion or estimate of one's importance." Maybe some of us feel as though we have no choice in saying yes or no to anything, which makes us feel less than necessary. Being modest does not mean not having any sense of self-importance, just not so much as promoting arrogance, vanity, and gigantic ego. As we progress in an area, we can step into pride if all we think of is ourselves and what benefits we can get individually instead of how our gifts can help so many more people.

Humility, for Christians, means believing what Jesus reminds us of in John 15:5: "Without me, you can do nothing!" Without our consistent, daily connection to Christ, we are ALL *one slip up away from sinning*. We may think we're doing well, but once we step out in our own power, all it takes is one wrong decision, one poor choice, and boom, we have sinned. Without the Holy Spirit and His grace and mercy surrounding us, we will become prideful. We need to take time regularly to honestly confront the areas in our lives that need growth, trusting that God has forgiven us and will equip us to grow in those areas. Honesty and growth are so refreshing! And once we trust in God and care for ourselves enough to reach new levels, we can experience God-fidence.

I see God-fidence as the integration of confidence, faith, and humility. Confidence is birthed out of consistency, faith is a deliberate choice, and humility is thinking of yourself less. All three together are vital so we can prioritize our self-care to be the very best version of ourselves for others. We know we have God-fidence when we have no bitterness from doing too much for others. Our faith guides our decisions to know that God brought about a divine opportunity to use us through the gifts He's given us. Humility helps us remember moment by moment that, without Christ, we are nothing. Let us be kind to ourselves by placing ourselves in an environment where we can talk honestly through our journeys with other like-minded people, such as in a small group.

3. Kindness is Contagious

Dr. Haidt, a professor of Psychology at The University of Virginia, found that people performing kind acts and those who witness them experience similar benefits. All involved get a rise in oxytocin, the "love hormone," in their brains, but the likelihood for the onlooker to do something kind themselves also skyrockets! The process is called Moral Elevation. When we take a moment to focus on others and do something for them, giving out of our abundance of time, money, and resources, our actions become contagious.

I will always remember when one year we went to a nice restaurant to celebrate my wife's birthday. It was my wife, my mother- and father-in-law, our "bonus" daughter Brittany, and I. It was a night full of laughs and great conversation, a great evening all the way around! We spoke briefly with a couple at the next table, were cordial to them, and thought nothing of it when they got up and left before we did. Then the waitress brought the bill for the meal. She told us a couple who had been sitting nearby paid our bill in full, including the tip! We were in utter shock! We wanted to run out and thank them, but they were already gone, obviously not even seeking to be acknowledged. We asked ourselves, "Who does this type of thing these days?!" We talked about it all the way home and for days afterward.

Since then, my wife and I have set a goal to bless others, and we look for new opportunities to do the same. We have felt led to bless several people, and we also began consistently giving our servers at any restaurant we would go to with a substantial tip (35-50% tips, minimum). We have had so many great conversations with our servers.

We did not want to make a huge deal, but we knew from Brittany sharing her stories of working as a waitress how many people would give an embarrassingly stingy tip, if anything at all. We wanted these servers to know there are still kind people out here who tip well. Servers have responded in various ways, such as crying, cursing in shock, and thanking us over and over. They opened up and shared their life stories with us when they realized how much their tip was. We are not rich yet, but we believe if people, especially Christians (and yeah, I'll go ahead and say it, people of color) were to be better financial stewards, we could give extraordinary tips, pay for others' entire meals, and bless with money in countless other ways. These kinds of acts can change a person's or family's outlook for the day, week, and even year. Dare I say their whole lives! And it has been so much fun! When we do act in kindness, not for others to see, but indeed from our hearts, we can cause a ripple effect of kindness, which can change our community and make us feel great as well. A true win-win!

4. Prevent anxiety and depression

Our world is becoming more and more addicted to everything from social media, fast food, opiates, and multiple sexual partners, to marijuana, cocaine, excessive gaming, and countless other things. These artificial substitutes are simply not filling the void in our lives. Kindness can make a huge difference to help people stop looking outside of themselves to find real joy and satisfaction. The Mesolimbic System is the part of our body that is responsible for producing natural hormones such as serotonin and oxytocin, which both release into our brains, causing us to feel a sense of love and reward. We mentioned this briefly when we talked about Moral Elevation and how this system is activated, both when we see and do something kind.

I truly believe many fall into major depression and anxiety because so many people, especially our youth and young adults, are looking for meaning and identity in their lives and have not found it. The easy way many have found to curb the sadness, emptiness, and pain is to use the substances mentioned above. Could the life-changing power of kindness be a suitable replacement to help fill the void inside? Kindness is scientifically proven to naturally produce the hormones that these other harmful and destructive habits and substances aim to do.

What if these hurting people could not only experience the power of kindness but also have the opportunity to understand the purpose of their lives? When you can learn, gain experience and start a career that is perfectly fitted for your personality, gifts, and dreams, there is no better feeling in the world! Kindness can help them start the journey to their true purpose.

5. Increase self-confidence and social awareness

When we have our minds set on kindness and how amazing it is for ourselves and those we help, we gain a superior confidence level. We begin to accept ourselves and believe we have something beneficial to give to others. Feeling fulfilled and satisfied in this life will provide us with that confidence. This is the confidence that will help us get up every morning, ready to attack the day and accomplish the goals that will get us closer to our dreams.

I believe kindness has the power to awaken a desire in us to want better for ourselves and those around us. As we move toward becoming kinder, more confident people, those around us will want the same for themselves. We become more and more aware of those around us and begin to strategize small ways to show kindness to them. Whether or not we let one, two, or three people into our lane, even though they waited until the LAST minute, we looked out for them. We all dislike traffic, but we always remember the kind people who let us in when we desperately needed to get home to whatever issue was waiting there for us. Kindness helps us become more in tune with who we are and what surrounds us, and it also helps to relieve the stress of life. This break, even for just a moment, can help stem the tide of negativity that we face daily. Even in the little moments, kindness matters!

Once we have fully experienced the life-changing power of kindness, our perspective on life, others, and ourselves dramatically improves! We begin to see life with a glass-half-full view instead of a glass-half-empty one. Kindness opens the door to many experiences that are beneficial to our self-esteem, our outlook, and even our physical health. Kindness can even enhance our life quality and increase our life expectancy. In her book *Raising Happiness: In Pursuit of Joyful Kids and Happier Parents*, Christine Carter states:

> "People who volunteer tend to experience fewer aches and pains. Giving help to others protects overall health twice as much as aspirin protects against heart disease. People 55 and older who volunteer for two or more organizations have an impressive 44% lower likelihood of dying early, and that's after sifting out every other contributing factor, including physical health, exercise, gender, habits like smoking, marital status, and many more! Believe it or not, but this is a stronger effect than exercising four times a week or going to church."

These attributes are mind-blowing to me! So, churchgoers, we cannot merely walk in and walk out of a church service regularly; we must get involved and serve to actually see these benefits!

When our lives have more opportunities to see and show kindness to others, our bodies respond positively. Our bodies release serotonin, a neurotransmitter that gives us feelings of happiness, relaxation, and one of the essential things in this world, a restful night's sleep.

It is time for each of us to stretch out and exercise our kindness muscles. Some of us have never even considered the slightest desire to be kind to others. In this cutthroat dog-eat-dog world, many of us have never found how exhibiting kindness, both in our profession and in our personal lives, can benefit us much, much more than stepping on the throats of whoever is in our way to what we deem success. I know specific skills and abilities get us into the building, but I believe kindness will take us to the top!

When you return to the gym after you have not been in a long time, you start slowly and work your way up so that your muscles have time to build and grow. I believe it is the same with kindness. Start with low-hanging fruit to get the ball rolling and create positive momentum to help you realize how incredibly beneficial kindness is. All of the hard work, soreness, sweaty gym clothes, protein shakes, early morning workouts, and Biofreeze (the new school Bengay) will pay off. Kindness always has and always will pay off too.

Chapter 6
Professional Communication Skills

I have been involved in church ministries in some way or another for over 23 years, and at times I believe it is on par with the business meetings and interactions at top corporations. Some people are desperate for control and power regardless of where the meetings occur. You don't need to look too far to recognize those who are willing to do any and everything to get what they want. Those with this aggressive, cutthroat mindset even exist in the church, but the solution to how we treat them is the same: kindness.

> Kindness means clarifying expectations from the jump.

At these meetings, you will find those who are on boards and committees only to help meet the quota to be able to call a vote. They are literal yes men and women who agree and vote with the majority every single time. We nice guys and gals tend to be the most consistent. We are dependable, showing up on time to each meeting, only to sign in and vote quietly, never to disagree or ruffle any feathers. I know from personal experience that we have a lot of opinions and great ideas that could make waves if we chose to share. But sadly, we stay silent, which is destructive to the overall goal.

Kindness Defined

I played this role more times than I care to admit. I have simultaneously worked in ministry and the educational/technology field for almost 20 years. I had stayed on the sidelines when vital decisions were occurring where I worked. I witnessed thousands of dollars be used to purchase technology equipment when I knew which would be the best options to consider, but many times I kept quiet without the confidence to speak up. My input could have saved the school and the district near hundreds of thousands of dollars in the long run if I had spoken up!

We neglect our duty when we do not share when it could make a difference. If I knew someone could save me lots of money and did not share it with me, I would definitely be upset about it! We, as nice guys and gals, have to look at our constant silence as harmful more times than not. We all make mistakes and sometimes make the wrong call, but that is not a reason to permanently stay silent! Instead, we can do more research and consult other more experienced people to see where our reasoning in our decisions fell flat so that we can grow from it. Withdrawing into our shells is not a kind position to stay in!

Many in corporate America have never considered how kindness can help them to rise to the top of their organization. There are not only kindhearted individuals but godly people in every company. Many are nervous about rocking the boat, about revealing how they believe and want to live out the spiritual principles they believe in, or maybe think others will not see the validity of it. But trust me, kindness always has and always will stand out!

In the wake of the #MeToo movement, people throughout the movie and music industries and also corporate America have been exposed. Their selfish, vicious, and unrelenting climbs to the top have come to light. While stepping on everyone else, they have destroyed families, taken whatever they wanted from others, and engaged in sexually manipulative acts that have deeply wounded countless people. Due to the power some of these individuals possess, they have gone unchecked for decades. But now, their house of cards has come tumbling down.

God put this quote on my heart: "Talent, smarts, and ability may get you in the door, but *character* will take you to the top!" The world has recognized that those without character are not capable of leading without leaving numerous women, men and families destroyed in their wake. Character in leadership is the only way to sustain a company's success long term, not only to make money but to help families, assist those who are less fortunate, make an impact in local communities and do so many other beneficial things! Leaders with character, who choose to take advantage of situations for their gain but choose not to, can propel a company towards being truly successful long term. Leaders can transform the culture of their entire organization by how kindly they treat those they don't have to treat well at all.

A major aspect of displaying character involves how we communicate. I realize I can often be long-winded when voicing my ideas instead of getting straight to the point. I have to constantly remind myself, "*Osei, this is no time for small talk.*" How many of our conversations would change instantly if only both sides involved would communicate clearly? I mean, if we were able to be crystal clear in terms of information and details so that there was absolutely no reason for anyone to be confused or to not know what happens next? I cannot think of many things more frustrating than to have a conversation with someone and make decisions based on that conversation, only to find out the other person interpreted things completely differently. Too many times in these types of conversations, the details were assumed unnecessary, when communicating them would have saved a lot of time, money, and resources. When we do not communicate clearly, relationships are strained, companies lose money, and frustration can overflow into heated interactions. When we do not share and communicate what is needed in a work environment when it is required, chaos is inevitable. Professional communication skills are vital, especially when money is involved.

Let us break down why communication is often unclear and then tackle some specific and practical ways to reach an understanding.

1. Fear of hurting the other person's feelings

Fear of hurting someone's feelings might be the number one cause of miscommunication. We sometimes feel what we have to say might offend or make the other person uncomfortable, and fear causes many of us to hide or parse out some of the necessary details from our side of the conversation. When it comes to communication, the *how* is more important than the *what*. Sensitive information shared in our conversations can understandably be difficult to handle. How we communicate and receive this sensitive information will determine what solution we should use.

Communicating clearly and stating the pertinent facts is vital to truly resolve an issue. For example, not explaining the details of how an employee could better meet necessary standards not only hinders the company but hurts the employee. Telling them exactly what you expect allows them the opportunity to see their areas of growth and begin to pull in resources to help them improve. A great leader or manager will be able to suggest tips and give their employees the necessary support they need to win and succeed, which will ultimately help the company go to the next level.

2. Not having all the facts or information

Say you have a crucial team meeting coming up to determine how much money to spend on a specific project and the group or individual responsible for bringing the key details does not have the information ready in time for the meeting. We won't get into whether or not they had all the resources, contacts, and background knowledge made available to them. The key is whether or not this person will share the disappointing but important fact that they are not ready for the meeting.

Avoiding arguments, frustration and confusion is a "nice" goal. Are they willing to simply communicate the situation ahead of time and look to reschedule once they have everything needed to have a successful meeting? Or will they choose to "be nice" and come to the meeting with, at best, incomplete information? Not communicating clearly, especially about having all the necessary facts and details, can make or break a company.

I believe the challenge lies in how comfortable employees feel in sharing disappointing information with their bosses. Every one of us makes mistakes, but most of the time, the real issue is not the mistake, but how quickly the error is recognized and a solution is implemented. Managers need to develop a strong rapport with their employees, so the lines of communication are open for them to discuss the situation regardless of the mistake. I believe most people would appreciate the openness and willingness of their boss to hear about problems along with potential solutions that they have to offer. The average boss will allow the frustration of the situation to push them to penalize or fire the employee responsible. Still, I believe showing kindness to that employee will be of more value and create a culture of overall success.

There is an expense associated with having to fire and then hire a new employee or a whole team. The downtime while the company is below capacity and the training involved to bring new staff up to speed is exponentially more costly than having a sit-down meeting with current employees and giving them the space to discuss challenges and solutions. This model does not allow for sanctioned incompetence (when negative, mediocre work or results are tolerated by those in charge) but encourages a culture of kindness. Employees behave differently in a company where expectations are crystal clear and where they receive kind and direct correction to help them be successful in their roles.

3. Not knowing how to share information kindly

Knowing how to share information kindly is a challenge that deals with tact. Dictionary.com lists tact as "a keen sense of what to say or do to avoid giving offense; skill in dealing with difficult or delicate situations." How do we say difficult things to those who need to hear what we have to say? Our tone, timing, and setting make all the difference, especially when the goal is kindness!

To have real, healthy, and growing relationships, we need to take some personal time to critically analyze our goals for all of our conversations. Do we always want to be heard? Do we just want to be right? Both of these mindsets can prevent continued conversations and disrupt relationships. Great relationships require give and take, and for a relationship to work, both parties must be willing to stop and listen. So many times, though, one or both parties claim they are listening when they are just being nice, and they have no idea what the other person is honestly saying. How many of us feel encouraged and heard when the other person takes the time to understand our concern or issue before they go into how to resolve it? We expect that kind of communication from doctors and mechanics, but is it difficult for us to genuinely listen to our loved ones first before we speak? How we talk to others can be one of our most significant displays of kindness!

I believe stress heightens in the workplace due to the often high levels of pressure and the expectations that come along with our jobs. As a leader, you can be a source of positivity and encouragement when you share things with your employees in a kind way. Just like when someone pays for your food at the drive-thru, it's hard to forget that boss or coworker who treats you kindly, especially when reprimanding you or even when letting you go.

A great leader knows how to put a personal touch on great communication. Doing things such as leaving employees a handwritten note in their mailbox or on their desk acknowledging the hard work they put in on a recent project could be a tremendous form of encouragement for them. Also, publicly praising someone who went above and beyond in their presentation could be a huge boost to their morale.

Additionally, it is a great tool for you to have your company or team take a personality assessment such as the Enneagram, D.I.S.C, or Love Language assessments to know best what form of acknowledgment each person would prefer. This speaks to taking the time and truly communicating love to them, which will be a great deposit in their emotional tank insterad of a withdrawal. My dominant love languages are Physical Touch and Words of Affirmation, so an appropriate hug or pat on the back along with a written note or email would be really encouraging to me specifically. I kept a lot of the notes of appreciation I received from the parents of the young people when I was their Youth Pastor. When I need a boost, I go back and read them again to remind me of the great work I was able to do in their lives. We can have the same effect, especially as leaders, to not only keep production high but acknowledge the person as well—a real gamechanger!

Being a Kind Employee

When we have a boss, we are paid to accomplish certain tasks and achieve specific goals. Many of us reading this now are blessed to have great jobs that we have enjoyed for many years, but even so, there will always be challenges on the job. There will be situations we need to address and conversations that we need to have. There will be uncomfortable moments where we do not prefer how someone else does something in relation to us being able to do our job. What do you do? Too many of us will remain silent. We won't address the issues we have with someone's work performance style, tone, demeanor, or whatever it is that hinders our ability to accomplish what we are expected to do. This can apply to our coworkers as well as to our managers. What do we do when we have an issue with someone at work, and we want to remain kind?

When we do not find a way to address our issues, our work suffers, and we will eventually begin taking our frustration with us when we leave work. This disappointment will naturally spill out onto those closest to us, at home, and in close personal relationships. These silent problems will affect our emotions and how we view work. We will begin dreading going to work, knowing that the issue will be waiting for us every day, lingering for weeks, months, and, tragically, for some, even years.

Here are a few ways we can address our issues at work both professionally and kindly:

1. Keep the tone 100% professional

We must make sure that we focus on our specific roles and duties, removing any and all personal feelings or even barbs out of our language when we share challenges with the person directly or with other parties. So many times, *how* we share our concerns is pivotal to our getting the resolution we want. If we are harsh, rude, critical, or demeaning in any way, we will not accomplish the desired effect.

2. Continue to do our jobs with the same skill and diligence

Though difficult, we have to make sure that the issue has a minimal effect on our job performance. Obviously, we are bringing it up because it has now become an issue, but if it brings our job performance down to unacceptable levels and we have not done our very best to accomplish what we are expected to get done, our position may also be at risk. This is why we must always do our job with excellence, so if there are issues, they will not seem as if they are originating with us because our consistency in completing our tasks will speak for itself.

3. Have some suggestions ready

When we bring up the issue, we should have some potential options prepared on how things can be resolved in case we are asked. Many times, what we suggest will be an easier fit than what our manager or supervisor will have to come up with on the fly. Sure, they are responsible for helping fix the issue, but this makes us take the proactive approach that bosses always prefer! At least one or two solutions that we are personally ok with and have already thought through can be a surprising benefit to help not only fix the issue but make things even better moving forward.

4. Be willing to hear other solutions

As in Stephen Covey's Fifth Habit in his book *The 7 Habits of Highly Effective People*, it is vital that we are willing to continue the conversation believing that an even better third solution exists that could make things much better than believed! But if we are close-minded, only wanting our way, we stifle the creative interdependence that can be generated from this apparent issue.

It is all about our mindset as a professional who is getting paid to do a job well. I believe with this type of attitude and mindset, new doors will open up for us once we can get through this current situation if all is done so with kindness! Kindness can be surprisingly practical, professional, and proactive if we allow it to! Following these steps can help us remain kind and professional while dealing with issues that hinder our ability to do our best job. Life is too short to sit quietly and allow issues to continue.

Being a Kind Boss

Maybe you are the boss of many employees, and you have been asking yourself how to earn revenue, save money, and continue to innovate while making sure your employees remain productive. The common trend is to train employees with verbal threats, salary loss, demotions, and control, but is that genuinely sustainable? Maybe you have seen for yourself how negative company morale can not only slow down performance but lose millions of dollars in lost work hours. It all comes down to how the ship runs. Why not try using the power of kindness? Kindness is the best way to run a corporation.

Let me remind you all here that kind bosses are not weak! In fact, they are the exact opposite! Kind bosses are the ones who make legacies for generations. It is so important for leaders to exemplify kindness and create systems that mirror that behavior so that kindness is lived out by employees, teammates, and leadership as well. You do not have to allow your employees to get over on you by taking off, being rude, and giving average effort. Kindness can help you get the best from those who work for you. You have to be determined to change the life of your business culture in a practical and meaningful way so that it will last for generations!

So, where do you start? When your company can grow and make a real positive impact in the community, that's when you have something extraordinary. In his book *EntreLeadership*, Dave Ramsey cautions companies to have a very thorough and rigorous process when hiring people. Having multiple interviews and high standards, along with competitive wages, can help weed out those who are not ready to live up to the standards you have set. This way, much of the pain and frustration of having to hire new people can be avoided before they become costly challenges.

This is how companies can begin making significant impacts on their employees, and eventually, the community as well. Without lying, cheating, manipulating, or taking advantage of workers, we can do this with the power of kindness. This behavior will stand out from all the corporate fraud and greed and will attract the best talent to work harder and stay longer. The level of positivity will be through the roof as the life-changing power of kindness will be exhibited from the CEO to the janitor!

1. Communicate ahead of time

When you have issues or challenges that need addressing, information on how to resolve them needs to be communicated clearly. Leaders hoarding information for whatever reason teaches the employees or team that they are not intelligent or competent enough to handle it properly. Nobody wants to feel like that. Show your team or company that you respect them enough as individuals to communicate challenges that may be on the horizon. Allow them to share their thoughts and possibly their suggestions on how to make changes to turn things around. Of course, at this point in your company, you've already done the proactive and challenging work of hiring the right people initially.

If you want to take your company to the next level, you have to invest in people with character. You cannot expect the best from those who are only there to get a paycheck. Instead, you need individuals who take pride in whatever their hands touch. You'll know these individuals with integrity can be trusted with important information because you've seen the work they've put in to help your company win.

Communicating with others ahead of time helps to spread the responsibility of success to everyone, not just one person. It is a great feeling to show up to work on a Monday morning, excited to be part of a winning team. There is a time and place for everything, and it's important to use discretion when distributing information. When we keep vital information secret when we don't need to, I believe we undermine the overall direction of the business or ministry because we can only go as far as our weakest link. Creating an open communication style takes time and investment, but the returns are endless, giving the company legs on which to walk into multiple generations. We've seen multi-million-dollar companies that are passed down to their children all the time; why not for us?

2. Be Clear and Direct

Let us go directly to one of the hardest aspects of running a company: when it is time to let go of someone. Other, less tense decisions like which color theme to choose for the website, what the company Christmas gift will be, and which type of chair to have in your office do not have a long-lasting impact.

Problematic employees consistently show their disregard for the policies, procedures, and principles that you have established for the company. Most of the time, it is easy to see who they are because their bad attitude, unwillingness to communicate, or their tendency to simply ignore their responsibilities have made them stick out like a sore thumb. It is time to show kindness and relieve them of their employment, so it is time to have an awkward conversation.

When you are having challenges with an employee, what stops you from approaching them early to restate your expectations of them in their role? Is it laziness? Are you afraid of their response? Your silence isn't being kind at all. We are kind when we are consistent, clear, and direct with our expectations, not micro-managing but instead reminding employees of their responsibilities. When bosses see these things occurring and do nothing, Dave Ramsey calls this "Sanctioned Incompetence" in his book *EntreLeadership*, which has no place in a thriving environment. Many of us quickly lose sight of our goals, vision, and purpose without a constant reminder.

THE CONVERSATION

When it is time to address a problematic employee, you can use the Sandwich Method, which means to share with the employee what they are doing well, then state the problem and thereafter end the conversation with a solution. Allow them to honestly share their point of view on your challenge. Misunderstandings of a particular role and responsibility in the company or position happen occasionally. This conversation can help clear the air and give that employee a clearer vision for their role in the company, increasing their dedication and focus, which is a win for everyone! It takes courage to have this awkward conversation, but it is a true act of kindness. Most employees will appreciate this treatment from the beginning so that they are aware of the situation.

Now, let us say that you have had multiple conversations with this employee; you have come up with written suggestions for how they can improve, but for whatever reason, it has not worked, and it is time now to let them go officially. Kindness does let people go.

Conversations about termination need to be crystal clear and direct. Maybe something along the lines of, "Thank you for your time here with us, but we have to let you go. We hope your next position will work out better for you." When we have already had previous conversations, developed a plan to help this employee readjust to their roles and responsibilities, and things still do not turn around, the final discussion will be brief. There should be no surprises for them about how you have come to this decision.

The problem can end up being a huge blessing for both parties, believe it or not. If proper interviewing and screening for this position were not done originally, that person might have never been able to succeed there, based on their personality and skills. Once they are removed from their role it reveals an opportunity to clarify the role and give this person the freedom to choose another role, better suited for them. This is what can be termed "Addition by Subtraction," which your company has probably needed for a long time.

Sometimes on certain teams, a talented individual can hinder the overall team's production. To get the most out of the team, that individual must be removed. It is time for a member of the team to be removed if they get away with having a bad attitude, showing up late, and not cooperating with everyone. This removal will help bring the team back together, calibrate roles and responsibilities, and give anyone who has any questions or suggestions the opportunity to share. Transitions can be difficult, but they can also be refreshing.

Removing or reassigning someone does not always have to be for a negative reason. Sometimes adjusting to one person's open role can be the breakthrough everyone needs. Giving them more opportunities to use their gifts in a needed location can bring fresh inspiration. Again, how we share the new opportunity will frame the situation moving forward.

Hopefully, we are the type of leaders that truly have an open-door policy where everyone feels comfortable sharing what they do not agree with or think could be done better or more efficiently. Creating a safe space to express frustrations and successes can ensure the company does not miss out on that one idea or adjustment that could completely change the office atmosphere and performance.

We don't have to be the smartest person in the room. We don't have to be the one who comes up with all the ideas. The purpose of a team is so that you will not have to do it all yourself.

It is time for us, as leaders, to win, not only in revenue but in our culture. It's important to have high morale and efficient systems that can not only succeed when times are going well but are strong enough to sustain when the economy takes a turn or when key people leave.

Chapter 7
BEING KIND AND STILL RISING TO THE TOP

Ok, let's keep things one hundred percent real here. Most of us do not love the job we are currently working in. We might be willfully stuck in the same position or should have never taken it in the first place. Let me say to you that this is perfectly normal.

Feeling unable to progress in your current job makes you just like the majority of people in the workforce right now. But there are some important questions you need to ask yourself. Questions such as, "Am I here because I do not believe I deserve a better position?" Or "Have I gotten so comfortable making a certain amount of money that now I am fearful of seeking a promotion where I'd have to legitimately work?" Or "Am I worried about seeming money-hungry to others?" Honesty with yourself is vital here because, as we know, being kind to yourself is the ultimate kindness. Today is the day to rid ourselves of these excuses.

> Talent, smarts, and ability may get you in the door, but CHARACTER will take you to the top!

Why are many of us so content with being and having less than we should? An important note, especially for the shy people who

Kindness Defined

are hesitant to put themselves in a position to be noticed, is that just because we want to be the best does not mean we think others are inferior!

We should want to be the best version of ourselves, not in comparison to others, but because God gets the most glory from our lives when we meet our promise (not potential)! Sadly, many of us are outwardly compliant while inwardly resentful. We remain afraid to apply for new positions, to interview at new companies, or to make our desires known. What exactly are we afraid of? Afraid of hurting our coworkers' feelings? Afraid of the seemingly overwhelming new responsibilities and expectations? With any new position, it takes time to acclimate. The challenge comes when we never try to push ourselves to be great because all we want is to be nice.

One of our biggest challenges is to honestly assess how much longer we will live a life beneath our abilities while knowing that our gifts and talents can do so much more. We go to work bored to tears, daydreaming of the level we want to reach. We dream of the ideal career opportunity, but we make excuses not to pursue it. We allow ourselves to rationalize away our present opportunities, focusing on all the reasons to stay where we are instead of focusing on all the reasons to go for it. An old Chinese proverb says the best time to plant a tree was 20 years ago, but the second-best time is now!

When we start a job or a career, we should want to be the best in our field! God's Word declares in Deuteronomy 28:13 that He wants us to be "the head and not the tail." What does this mean for us? It starts with our mindset or work ethic and the belief that God wants us to be the head. As long as we honor Him in all our decisions, He will promote us into places of influence so we can better help and serve others. Jesus served us by owning and living out who He was, the Savior of the world, to set us free.

It's a subtle deception to think that we are pious by not wanting better for ourselves and our future. We often believe the lie that God is satisfied with us being average. Just as the clay will harden when it just sits in the sun, if we stay still, not purposefully growing and maturing, we can harden our hearts and easily slide into sin over and over again.

So many of us are skilled and educated in various fields, but we take the easy way out. We ride our talent towards finding a job to pay the bills and take care of ourselves, our families, and our responsibilities. These are all noble aspirations, but what about the spiritual gifts God has given us? The Bible says in 2 Timothy 1:6 that we are to "stir up the gift." The next verse goes on to say, "For God has not given us the spirit of fear, but of power and of love and of a sound mind." Our gifts are not meant to be left on the bench or stored somewhere on a dusty shelf! Ideally, we are to put them to use so that God will get the glory, and we will be truly fulfilled in using this tailor-made gift fitted just for us. God loves us so much and knows us so well. We need to trust God and move forward!

I mean, honestly, what kind of life are we living if we're satisfied to get a check, but every day we're just going to work to watch the clock? We need to be kind to ourselves and accept who we are in Christ. Being kind to ourselves will allow us to use the gifts He has given us. True Christianity will enable us to step back and let Him open and close doors as He sees fit! There are life lessons we need to learn to grow to where God wants us to be, but we must be willing to push to the top of our fields, use our gifts, and learn those initially uncomfortable but ultimately helpful life lessons to increase our joy and connection to God!

The Kindness Breakthrough

When we choose to be nice instead of kind at work, we can become bitter. Maybe we know in our hearts that we are fully capable of doing a better job than our current manager or boss. We have ideas and initiatives that could completely transform our company for the better. Regrettably, we continue to keep our suggestions to ourselves. We are working hard but not smart, and we look at our situation daily, knowing it could be much better. We choose not to say anything about it while the bitterness steadily increases in our hearts, eventually leaving us boiling mad on the inside. I cannot imagine anything more frustrating than this!

We must take the time to process what is inside of us stops us from expressing our thoughts and ideas. What would help us work smarter and enhance our impact? Are we concerned about what will happen to our boss if we seem to outdo them? Or do we believe that when we bring up great suggestions or ideas, we will be considered a "brown nose"? If we are honest with ourselves, maybe we lack confidence in our abilities and believe we wouldn't be able to handle it if we did get promoted. Maybe we think we would somehow mess everything up, and the expectations on us would be too high for us to be comfortable.

All of these scenarios speak to deep-seated insecurities that reveal themselves through people-pleasing. We allow the weaknesses, shortcomings, or vulnerabilities of others along with our own weaknesses to stifle our growth. Some of us have been at or below middle management positions for so long that we have gotten comfortable. But our comfort is leaving us vulnerable to have the newly hired person come in and steal our ideas, share them with the decision-makers, and take the position destined for us. Kindness involves pushing ourselves to get what we deserve! It involves using our ideas, gifts, and suggestions to the best of our abilities, which will help us live life to the fullest. Pretending that it doesn't bother us when our great ideas are continually ignored is just being nice.

It might be time to straight-up leave and move on to another, a better opportunity where we'll be more appreciated. Starting a business of our own may be another possibility. Life is too short, and there are so many opportunities out there for problem solvers. We need to choose to believe in ourselves and use our God-given abilities how He wants to see them manifest!

God wants His people to be in positions of influence to be able to help others and, at the same time, have true fulfillment, satisfaction, and joy. The story of Joseph in the Bible, in Genesis 37-47, is one of my favorite Bible stories and directly relates to what I am sharing with you. Joseph was a young man who had a dream. No one in his family believed in the dream, or him for that matter. He was betrayed by his brothers and thrown in prison, and he thought his life was over. He chose to believe in the One who gave him his dream and live under His will, even while jailed! Through his faithfulness to God and using his gifts while holding firm to his principles, he was able to positively impact his jailors and others in prison, eventually making room for him to guide the then-known leader of the world! Joseph was able to wisely counsel the Pharaoh on how to save the entire nation and also saved his own people from dying in the famine. Joseph's story shows what I believe God wants to do for us, to be in key positions to help as many people as we can to see God's power and get to know Him better. It is time for us to banish fear and step into the role God has ordained for each one of us to operate in!

Stepping into that new role might not be easy. How many things are not fun for us initially but are ultimately beneficial for us? We know getting in shape is one of the hardest things we need to do, but once we get there, everything in our lives is better! Our health, sleep, and our ability to stay alert improves; we recover faster from injuries, and the list goes on. But to get the results, we have to start the process.

And I truly believe it begins with our young people. While children are young, parents should be praying and asking God to reveal what their children's gifts are so they can support them in these areas. They should prayerfully consider where those gifts will have the best trajectory, where God can get the most glory from it, and where their children can be truly fulfilled and have fun. And, above all, they should demonstrate and encourage a daily, consistent relationship with God!

Chapter 8
KINDNESS AND MONEY

Money. Money. Money. We all need it to survive. We have to use money for our essential needs like food, clothes, and shelter. How we spend and save money shows a lot about our character. We use cash for basic needs, for simple luxuries, and for larger unwise purchases that can leave us in significant debt.

Money can cause a lot of stress, but I'll say it now: Money itself is not evil! The Bible states in 1 Timothy 6:10 that "the love of money is the root of all evil." Just like a brick can be used to build part of a hospital, it can also be used to shatter a car window to steal a purse on the seat. The determining factor is whose hands the brick is in.

> Kindness always multiplies itself every time.

What type of character do we show when we handle our money? How many of us give money to what we would consider worthy causes? Do we support our local church, a charity, or families in need? Do we feel the need to do so?

I believe that there is a spiritual principle about money that applies to everyone. Luke 16:10 says, "He that is faithful in little will also be faithful in much." So many Americans (including myself) are terrible at managing money wisely. Too many of us live beyond our means with credit cards to buy things we don't need to impress people we don't like. How we feel about ourselves is seen mainly in how we spend our disposable income—the funds left after we pay for our basic needs.

A lot of people donate to charitable organizations. Many others follow the principle of tithing as the ten percent we give helps the church continue to share God's love with the world. I'm exhorting all Christians to take their giving to the next level. God promises in Luke 6:38 that if we "Give, and it shall be given to you."

I see this as where the power of kindness can significantly move the needle in our lives and help others at the same time. God blesses us with financial resources, not just for us to use but also to give. You may have had an opportunity to bless someone with financial help, seen how grateful that person was, and felt blessed as well. When we allow God to use us to bless others, we are also blessed! We can share these blessings beyond tithing and making donations.

I feel passionate about calling out many of us Christians who are just awful tippers! I'm talking about the entitled, and judgmental Christians who flat out refuse to give a generous tip, and not just the standard 15-20 percent society has guilted us into giving. The waiters, waitresses, and stewards who serve us have to take care of themselves and their families. Many of us here in the U.S. are ridiculously blessed, and we won't feel a hit to our wallets with a 25%, 35%, or even a 50% tip. We may say arrogant things as excuses like, "Well, they should get a better job," or "He or she was rude and didn't get my order perfect, so I won't give them a substantial tip." This is embarrassing to me. We caused this problem, and it is time for us to turn it around.

Let me pause here and say something to those Christians who say they can't afford to give a generous, eye-popping tip each time they go out to eat. I have a simple, basic solution for you: Stay Home! Eat at home and make a deliberate plan to pay off your debts so you won't be affected in the slightest by giving an abundant tip on the occasions you go out and when you get food delivered to your home.

I believe that we should tip more, especially when we get horrible service! The Bible says in Romans 12:20-21, "If your enemy is hungry, feed him; if he is thirsty, give him a drink; For in so doing you will heap coals of fire on his head. Do not be overcome by evil, but overcome evil with good." Now, I'm not saying the waiter who gives you attitude, or lousy service is your enemy or that what he did to you that night was evil, but the principle here is that we as Christians are not called to respond the same as we are treated! I'm basically saying that if someone is rude to you, you are not supposed to be rude to them.

What will make us stand out from others? What will allow us to share God's love with others? When they give us evil, we choose to provide them with kindness! I know this is not easy. I cannot stand to get terrible service, to be treated rudely, or to have my order come out wrong. The challenge is, how do we show kindness regardless of how we are treated? The server may eventually acknowledge that they were rude to you. But how you respond, especially when the check comes, makes all the difference.

It's common to see stories on the news or on social media of a patron who gets terrible service, gives the server a rude and low tip, and even writes some "advice" on the bill receipt. That service person takes a picture and posts it online for all to see. If the customer was someone famous, their reputation is then tarnished just because they wanted to make a point.

Be honest with yourself. Do you believe that that service person will accept advice when you embarrass them? Wouldn't it be kinder to bless them with a ridiculous tip, and see how they respond afterward? The most essential part of all of this challenge is that we have no clue what other people have gone through or are currently going through. How dare we judge that person strictly on the one time we interacted with them, without even a thought to pray for them, especially when we are getting bad service?

Kindness Defined

Almost every time my wife and I have gone out and given a generous tip to our server, they opened up, and we got a glimpse of what was currently going on with them. My wife, Antoné, is a sanguine (very outgoing type, never met a stranger), so she is often willing to spark up these conversations. We've heard how one server's ex wouldn't pay child support and how another needed extra money to pay their rent for the month. We have even heard from one waiter that no one else had tipped them that entire day!

Christians, do we care enough about the precious soul that Jesus went to the cross and died for to accept their poor attitude, pray for them, and choose to bless them regardless of how we are treated? Where is our compassion, to look away from ourselves, past the lousy service to see someone who God loves?

I believe we hesitate to tip because we have not been wise enough financially to create enough margin between our bills and our generous gifts. If you have a real challenge with this concept, you may need to sit down with a pastor or a professional counselor and talk through it. If you are just a nominal Christian and see a problem with this, something is missing spiritually, and I will not apologize for challenging you. I know people have treated us wrongly, I get that. But the server you're interacting with does not know that.

I've seen from personal experience that when we choose to be kind and bless those who serve us, we can be a light to them and point them to Jesus by how we treat them.

To be clear, if you have a specific issue, like if your waiter ignored your warning about a peanut allergy or claims you never mentioned it, you might need to speak with a manager instead of just ignoring it. I'm not an advocate for Christians being doormats. We should not respond to ill-treatment with more yelling, screaming, and cursing, but sometimes we do need to speak up. We can pray, stay calm, and communicate clearly. And once the smoke settles, we can still give a generous tip.

Givers and Takers

During my years at Howard University, I had a fantastic summer job as a lifeguard at an indoor pool in Adams Morgan. I had my parents' old brown Ford Taurus to get me to work, to school, and back. It had a leaky radiator that I had to fill up on my way to work and on my way home. I worked alongside five other lifeguards. We were never short on drama in the surrounding neighborhood and among the staff. There were guys from the area bringing guns into the indoor pool, fellow lifeguards bringing guns to work with them, and lifeguards having "friends" in the neighborhood, but I loved it. I loved everything about working there, except for the possibility of a gunshot wound.

At one point, one of the other lifeguards, we'll call him Dwayne, asked to borrow $200 from me until our next payday, which was two weeks away. Now Dwayne had a lot of drama. He had children with multiple women and was always making bad decisions, in my opinion. He seemed genuine most of the time, and I felt terrible for him, so I decided to loan him the money. That was the last I saw of it. He came up with excuse after excuse about how this woman wanted money from him for his daughter or how his car needed to get fixed (my car needed to be fixed too, Dwayne!), and so on. That summer ended, and I never got my money back from Dwayne even though he had insisted that he would pay me back.

After I graduated, I stopped working as a lifeguard. I met and started dating the woman who is now my wife, finally left my Mom's basement and bought a condo. A few months after moving in, who did I happen to run into again but Dwayne? And the first thing on my mind when I saw him? Where is my money!? I honestly can't remember if I brought it up when I talked to him, but it was definitely on my mind. That was three to four years after I had loaned the money to him. I learned then that loaning money to people is always a bad idea. Apart from drama and stress, the process causes arguments, strained relationships, and long-lasting bitterness.

Kindness Defined

Following the same principle I shared about tipping, I strongly believe that we as Christians should NEVER loan people money at all costs, especially when the family is involved. I have never seen a positive outcome from lending money. Either it will take much longer than agreed to for them to get you your money back, or you won't get it back at all. Then, more than anything else, it will return to the forefront of your mind when you see them again. Every great family event, every cookout, birthday, or holiday will turn sour. Your entire mood and thoughts will be on edge because of what occurred many years ago when you were trying to be nice. You should either give the money as a gift or say that you kindly cannot provide it at the moment.

The Bible says in Proverbs 22:7 that "the borrower is a servant to the lender." We become indebted to the person or company that we borrow money from. This system is popular throughout our country, especially in the housing and automobile markets. We lean on credit to increase our credit score so that loan providers will see us as a worthy investment while they make trillions off of our decisions. Now, I'm not against taking out a loan for larger items like cars and homes, but I believe it is time for Christians to dramatically improve our habits when it comes to our finances.

My wife and I have honestly made several terrible decisions with money in our marriage. We once bought a home water filtration system that ended up being a waste. And there was the timeshare that we only went to once but somehow are still paying off. We can testify to how living beyond our means and taking out loans with exorbitant interest fees is not the way to go. The Bible speaks multiple times about money and how we are called to be excellent stewards. In fact, Jesus Himself spoke more about money than any other subject aside from the Kingdom of God while He was here on earth.

Jesus is a giver. His purpose was to give His life as a ransom for every person ever born. During His life on earth, He was always on the lookout for people to help and provide them with encouragement, hope, healing and life. I believe that our lives will be more fulfilling and meaningful if we adopt how Jesus lived His life on earth. First, we have to change our mentality from that of scarcity to one of abundance and giving. Luke 6:38 says, "Give, and it shall be given unto you." Those who choose to apply this concept to their lives are blessed internally, knowing they did something for someone else outside of themselves.

Many of us who come from generations of low to mid-level income households have a scarcity, poor, and ghetto mentality. Growing up, my family and I were lower-middle class. We had an apartment and then eventually moved into a home. My dad worked hard but finances were tight. Being broke is a temporary situation but being poor is a mindset. We're taught not to spend any money, save everything and definitely never give money away to anyone. I believe we should save our money, especially in case of emergencies, but some of us go overboard in our mentality and become takers. Takers always ask things like, "What's in it for me?" or "What is the minimum amount of effort I can give to get what I want?" This is a poor mentality. It is a stronghold that we've built over our families and communities that perpetuates our crabs in a barrel thinking.

The cycle of scarcity exists in our inner cities. This financial haze has become a thick black cloud over our communities that suffocates the hearts of those who have lived there for generations. It's a place where great jobs always seem to be out of reach, which causes residents to hoard their meager incomes, and I believe it keeps them from getting out of this vicious cycle of being poor.

I believe with sound financial principles, being broke will only be a temporary condition as opposed to the perpetual poor mindset. We need to focus on attaining additional streams of income as a community of believers. We must begin to create a financial margin in our lives! Living from check to check is not the move to make. Yes, getting out of debt is essential, but if we do not have a bigger shovel, like say a larger salary or additional streams of income, to dig ourselves out, then we'll get stressed and eventually give up. In our world today, with the increasing access to technology, starting a small business could not be any easier! We do not have to quit our current jobs. We can begin doing a little bit after work. You can start reading, going to related seminars, and be rolling before you know it!

It is time for us to have something to hand down to our children, like a home, so they can build on a solid financial foundation for generations to come. Teaching them how to invest, or start a small business are also amazing gifts that will help our children to have multiple streams of income to be in a better position to provide for themselves and others.

Learning and being wise in our finances shows kindness to ourselves and to our families. When we are smart with our money, God can use us to bless our families and numerous other families that need a push to stop living from paycheck to paycheck. I'm not suggesting that we pay off all of their bills, but that we provide financial gifts and wisdom so they too can achieve financial freedom.

Chapter 9
Personal Communication Skills

How many of us have difficulty speaking up about things we do not like, do not agree with, or feel uncomfortable about? I mean simple things, like letting your boss know you would prefer a suite-mate or asking your coworker not to leave their window open, or telling them that their music is too loud. Whatever it is, are we able and willing to speak up about it? How much time will go by before we dare to bring up our concerns? The majority of the time, when we simply just go along to get along, no one even knows how we actually feel about things. It is possible to raise our concerns kindly and stop feeling silently frustrated and angry.

> Kind people give a pleasant 'no.'

We need to learn how to communicate clearly, not only on a professional level but on a personal, day-to-day level. Stephen Covey states as one of the key principles in his book *The 7 Habits of Highly Effective People*, that we should "Seek first to understand, then to be understood." Unfortunately, many people don't know how to communicate without shutting down completely or screaming, which only escalates the first issue to an unnecessary level. Even most families have some degree of dysfunction. It usually begins with the communication style we grew up seeing modeled by our parents, cousins, aunts, uncles, and grandparents and we carry those habits throughout our own lives. This history of dysfunctional communication is not a challenge if we are willing to acknowledge it and be prepared to learn better ways to communicate.

The Golden Rule states that we should treat others the same way we want to be treated. This directly applies to how we communicate with others. But let's back up for a minute. What does communicating kindly even look like? We interact with people from diverse backgrounds, so how do we apply this principle in different situations? Let's look at the various relationships that we tend to have the most challenges with, especially when it comes to having difficult conversations.

Immediate Family

Disagreements with family members can be some of the most confusing, stressful, and disappointing situations we experience. No family is perfect. Once we acknowledge that we are not part of a perfect family, we can speak directly to our challenges and come up with solutions to work through the frustration and misunderstandings that can ruin some of the most powerful family bonds.

When we speak to our children about their behavior, we tend to go to extremes. We might excuse their behavior or completely blow up at them, sometimes with a lot of fussing and cussing, and maybe in a demeaning way. These positions aren't sustainable long term. Kindness is key, but this does not mean we are pushovers. The goal is to be able to say no with a smile.

Children and teenagers need clear limits that make sense for their age and that will be strictly enforced in order for them to be ultimately successful as young adults and adults. The world outside of your home can be unforgiving if rules are not followed, so they must learn how to follow the rules before they have to fend for themselves. We must see our role as parents as vital to our children's success, especially during this time of increased bullying. When we teach our children to make their own decisions, make mistakes, and learn from them, we help them to build confidence as they grow, and they will be less of a target to bullies.

Sometimes, teens and young adults are the ones who need to speak up and communicate their concerns. Where they want to go to college, which career they want to focus on moving forward, and who they choose to date are topics that must be clearly addressed instead of stuffed away and denied. As parents, if we ignore these issues in favor of being nice, it may cause harm to those closest to us, our children. Instead, let's empower them to find their voice and they will first learn through our modeling. These are sensitive conversations, but I believe they can still be handled kindly.

Neighbors

Unless you happen to own all the houses in your area, there is no way to avoid having neighbors. The real question is how (the majority of kindness is about *how*) to interact kindly with people, especially when they are not the ideal neighbors.

I have a difficult time being around neighbors who do not consider other people. I tend to be overly focused on others, to the point where I might become too sensitive on this topic, but to me, it is simply rude not to consider those around you. Like when it comes to how loudly people play their music/televisions, or how fast they drive through a community and even if they know the community rules (official or unofficial) to follow.

Here are three ways to kindly address these challenges with your neighbors:

1. Know your community rules

This is a great practice to fully understand and know exactly what you and your neighbors are responsible for within the community. If you do not know for a fact, how can you legitimately get upset? Get all the information, so that you can confidently address your concerns with your neighbor.

2. Build connections

How you handle misunderstandings and uncomfortable situations points back to your character. How will you respond during negative situations? Will you keep your cool? Or will you hold in your frustration until you explode? There are several ways to react, but the goal is to simply be kind from the start. Smile and speak to your neighbors when you see them.

We all have issues and challenges in our lives, but are we going to allow our outside circumstances to determine how we treat ourselves and others regularly? Who has control in that situation? We need to take back control of our lives by being proactive and treating people as we want to be treated. When we are proactive, we start with being deliberate in making positive interactions with our neighbors and those in our communities to build bridges that we may need to cross over later due to a mistake or misunderstanding. On top of getting to know your neighbors and learning about their families, their careers, and their beliefs, being proactive will help provide a smooth foundation for when you do want to address a concern without having the conversation turn negative or combative.

3. Communicate Ahead of Time

When we are at the point where there is a clear issue that needs to be addressed, we should not wait to bring it up. We open the door for more problems when we do not speak about the issue promptly. Some situations with our neighbors are accidental, like when someone is in a rush and not able to clean up or put things back in place once or twice. But ongoing issues must be addressed.

You can start these conversations smoothly, like, "Can you please _____" or "When you get a chance, can you kindly _____?" On top of the rapport, you have already built, sharing your concern can help you resolve issues quickly. Now, if the situation still continues after multiple attempts to communicate, then it is time to begin documentation. Note the time, date, and location of the incident with whatever other pertinent details for when you need to pass the issue up. Some personalities will not comply with simple requests without significant "motivation." This doesn't mean you should lose your temper. You should just communicate the truth and allow the consequences to fall where they may.

Whatever consequences they receive due to ignoring the rules of the neighborhood are not our fault. Many times, we tend to not want people to experience the negative results of their actions. Some need to come to the realization that a more significant problem exists in their life to resolve. How we treat our neighbors is often how they will treat us. If all else fails, pass the issue up. If we fall back into being nice just to keep the peace, the problem will be unresolved, and the neighbor won't have the chance to grow.

Friends

Friends help make or break us in our lives. Jim Rohn, one of my favorite motivational teachers breaks down that we are the average of our five closest friends. Our friends help determine our level of success or failure in life, so we must choose them prayerfully and carefully! I see three categories of connections we have with others.

The first category is the casual acquaintance. You probably know this person's name, and maybe know where they live and work. You are cordial with them and make casual conversation, but that is as far as it goes. The next category includes people that we are attracted to in a romantic way and if you are not already married, then this person may be a potential spouse. You know what you are looking for in a spouse, and you are physically attracted to them. These are the individuals you want to get to know on a deeper level. The last category is that of a brother or sister in Christ. This is a person that you are not attracted to, a person whom you would be happy to pull back from if needed and who you would be happy for when they find their potential future spouse.

In regard to heterosexual dating, I believe men and women should not be friends but only brothers or sisters in Christ. Think about how much time, money, and emotional bandwidth are wasted when we try to lie to ourselves that a person of the opposite sex is simply a friend. By nature, we grow attracted to people of the opposite sex, especially the closer we get to them. When we pretend that this is not the case, we cause significant problems for ourselves. If a guy has a close female friend and finds a woman he is interested in, he will need to back up from being as close with his friend to ensure that the woman he is interested in knows she is number one in his life. It is time to be proactive and avoid having close friends of the opposite sex. That way, when you do meet that potential future spouse, you can focus without having to worry about hurting your friend's feelings.

I want to speak just to the men for a moment. I will be honest. I have made significant changes to ensure happiness in my home. I chose to remove specific cell phone numbers, online friends, and followers to protect myself from a potentially weak moment when I am not getting along with my wife and want to talk to a friend of the opposite sex for consolation. Marriages have ended on much less, but these situations are recipes for disaster! I have had to realize I am not responsible for other people's feelings and that my wife's emotional wellbeing is my number one priority. That realization made it much easier to cut ties with these other women.

These conversations are delicate to navigate, but ultimately there is no room to make excuses. If I need advice on how to work through a challenge my wife and I are having, I call my happily married brother, who understands what I am experiencing and can give me sound wisdom on how to resolve it. I know we are not perfect, and even a brother or sister in Christ can attempt to gain closeness that is not for them to have during a moment of weakness, but it's less likely when we set boundaries and have this mentality.

Now, ladies, welcome back. Real friends should not need anything from you. They shouldn't need our money, our clout, or anything that we may have. Great friends encourage and support you by choice because they care for you, and not for any other reason. They can be there for you, be a sounding board for you, help you carry life's burdens, and support you in whatever direction your life is heading. They visit you when you or your family are sick, help you move into your new home, and sit next to you while you grieve. These are the characteristics of a friend and when we are kind to our friends, we bring these same characteristics to the table and more.

Strangers

How we treat those we do not already know or who we do not *need* to treat kindly says a lot about our character. Most people will just be nice to strangers. We try not to bump into people while walking, we try not to step on their shoes, and we usually don't yell or scream at them. This is part of simply being polite. Kindness does more.

The University of California at Berkeley's Greater Good Science Center has proven that when we are kind to others, especially strangers, both parties experience benefits. Serotonin, a naturally occurring neurotransmitter, is released in our brains and gives us a sense of delight when we treat others kindly. Our world, society, and community are all becoming more cynical. We have grown oblivious to common courtesies, but even a simple kind act can easily make someone's day. I want to begin a movement of kindness, where we look for any and every opportunity to show kindness without wanting anything in return. With kindness, we could easily help warm the cold hearts and minds of so many in our world today.

Chapter 10
RELATIONSHIPS AND KINDNESS

Growing Up Nice

Let's talk about a nuclear American family: Dad, Mom, two children, and a dog. We'll call them the Nice Family. We see them going about their days like most other families. We might say, "What a nice family they are!" But let's dig a little deeper into this and reveal some of the challenges they may be susceptible to by being nice.

First, let's look at Dad – Maurice. Maurice loves his family and does what is necessary to take care of them as the breadwinner. He shows up to work on time every day, is diligent and hardworking. He never complains or disagrees. He keeps his head down, does his work well, and then goes home. But sometimes Maurice brings work home with him because his boss asks him at the last minute to complete tasks, which takes away from his time to spend with his family and to relax. He has excellent ideas for how things could run more efficiently and increase profits, but he stuffs it inside out of fear of rocking the boat. Maurice makes up excuses in his head like, "Well, they wouldn't understand it anyway" or "Things are ok, so

> Kindness implies confrontation when necessary.

there's no need to introduce a lot of changes now" or even, "Maybe I'll say something later."

Maurice's challenge is that he is too nice. He is a brilliant worker, but for some reason, he does not feel fulfilled in his position. He knows he can do more and offer more, maybe even start his own company, but he dismisses these ideas in order to keep the status quo. Maurice feels depressed and stuck but he's too compliant to share his feelings with anyone. The emotional space he is in sadly pushes him away from his wife and children.

Now, we have Mom, and her name is Keisha. She is a stay-at-home mom and works hard caring for their two children. Her challenge is that she always puts her children ahead of herself, neglecting exercise, personal quiet time, or even a hobby, all so that she can be with her children 24/7. She does all the disciplining, cooking, and cleaning, and helps with homework, all with a smile on her face. Occasionally her sister Carmen comes over to talk, but instead continually complains to Keisha about her own life. Although Keisha is busy, she always allows Carmen to continue with her emotional dumping. Her sister complains for hours without asking for or brainstorming any possible solutions. Carmen never even asks if Keisha wants to talk about what is going on in her life. Keisha is always tired, dreaming about when she and Maurice can get away for an actual vacation, but she banishes the thought from her mind, believing that when she ignores her own needs for others' that she is being a "good Christian."

Now let's talk about their children. First, we have Tristan. Tristan is an intelligent teenager, but he is timid and introverted. He makes mediocre grades even though he's smart and is an average player on his baseball team, though he's exceptionally athletic. He has lots of friends but does not know how to say no. When his friends ask him to go to places and do things he understands he shouldn't, he goes along with it anyway. Tristan agrees to whatever his group of friends says to avoid being the wet blanket. He often comes home late and skips doing any of his chores, mainly because he knows his mom will do them herself anyways. Josh struggles with low self-esteem and depression, never feeling like his friends will listen to his ideas and thoughts. He hides in a world of video games where he has some control but never dares to stand up for himself in the real world. Josh applies to where his parents want him to attend college, instead of the school that has the degree program he'd prefer. But, to avoid any conflict, he goes with his parents' choices to make them happy.

Finally, we have Lauren. She is four years old and has just started preschool. She enjoys playing and is a happy child, but her mom insists on her being nice and sharing, especially with her toys. Lauren has a problem with her friend Julie. Every time Lauren begins playing with her favorite toy, Julie starts asking for it over and over again, crying loudly until she gets an adult's attention in order to get what she wants. Keisha tells Lauren to comply to keep Julie from crying more and, as soon as Julie gets the toy, the crocodile tears vanish. While Lauren is young, she is already shaping how she will respond to situations for the rest of her life.

Let me say this right off the break, I am currently not a parent and have not yet had the benefit and privilege of raising children with my wife. Although we have our bonus daughter, Brittany, sadly my wife and I have experienced three miscarriages over the course of our marriage. I do have over 23 years of experience in youth ministry and going on 20 years teaching and working in technology with our local public school system. With each year that passes, technology continues to advance, and our families are breaking down right before our eyes. Whether you relate to the nuclear family or not, all families are struggling mightily, especially our children. I genuinely believe, aside from being President of the United States, being a parent in this generation is the most challenging job.

Kindness is introduced, modeled, and matured within the family. In a safe and nurturing environment, kindness can be instilled into our children, marriages, and extended family, in our churches, and then spread exponentially through our communities. Where else would we learn true kindness if not at home? Our schools are not built for this type of education. Our churches can confirm and give more avenues for practical experience with others outside the family, but it all begins at home.

The way we teach and model for our children how we are to treat others is vital in their emotional growth, confidence, and future success. What we instill in them is of paramount importance. This foundation is so important that I have to strongly disagree with the one statement I have repeatedly heard from parents when conflicts arise between children and their siblings or friends, which is "Be nice to _____." It sounds so innocent. Maybe you're thinking, "Isn't that what we should be telling them to do? It is our job to teach our children to be nice, right?" But what is that teaching them? Are we modeling proper conflict resolution? How we teach them to handle conflict will either form a firm foundation moving forward or create huge pitfalls of emotional weakness and even a fearful mindset towards any conflict. Let's look at some different relationship habits and break this down.

When Keisha told Lauren to "be nice" when Julie wanted the toy she was currently playing with, what message was she sending them? From what I see, it communicates to our children: *do not make any issues for me now. Outwardly comply so that you do not hurt the other person's feelings. I might get you what you want later but give up what you want for now.* There are numerous challenges in the story above that I would like to highlight.

1. It creates low self-esteem in our children

Each of us needs confidence, and our children need to develop a strong foundation in who they are and who they are not. Wise parents recognize this need and begin to reinforce their identity and worth as early as possible. These reinforcements might come through age-appropriate confidence boosters, such as noticing when they make excellent choices or when they naturally share without being forced. I see the results of children who have a low sense of worth and value, especially when they become teens like Tristan. They get involved in making all sorts of bad decisions, often to feel better about themselves. This life is difficult, but we can truly help our children to become confident and also to be kind. Children like Tristan have so much promise, but that potential can be squandered if not reinforced.

2. It encourages pretense and eventual bitterness

When we allow our faces and words to agree while our hearts disagree, we become a shadow of ourselves. Who we are as individuals shrinks when our thoughts and feelings go unexpressed. When we only outwardly comply, we will eventually inwardly resent. Like a blockage of built-up plaque in our veins, the hidden resentment will remain imperceptible until something terrible happens. This becomes problematic and potentially dangerous if allowed to continue and is reflected in our children.

Whether we want them to or not, children learn from how we interact with others and not being able to speak up for themselves leaves them susceptible to being taken advantage of and/or bullied. Once older, they will have learned to allow themselves to work for less than they're worth and be taken for granted in relationships, all of which is not a great way to prepare our children.

When we continue to go along to get along, our moral boundaries can start to get blurry as we bottle up our bitter and frustrated thoughts and feelings. I believe that holding emotional or spiritual challenges inside our hearts and minds is very destructive. When we try to keep things bottled up, we experience significant physical consequences. There are no expiration dates to spiritual and emotional issues. They must be identified and adequately addressed. Until we face our struggles, we will be involved in activities and situations that are counter to our morals, our identity, and our character.

The issue is that once we cross the line, we become con artists that can blend into any environment. We can see things going completely wrong and identify a solution, but still allow it to happen without ever feeling the need to speak up about it, never wanting to look like the bad guy, or to get people upset with us by rocking the boat. When we do not open up, our frustration, disappointment, thoughts, and emotions will build and eventually explode. And, more times than not, that explosion will hurt ourselves and those closest to us.

Our entire world would change if we were to realize that just being nice to people is not only annoying but potentially dangerous to our physical and emotional well-being. This concept sounds simple in theory, but it is difficult in practice. Instead of throwing pills at the situation, we could dig a little deeper with people. We could stop waving at the smoke, like the health issues, the lack of sleep, headaches, and depression, and we could get to the source of the fire, put that out, and feel better. It begins with kindness!

3. It invalidates their "NO"

When we learn to live out this people-pleasing and harmful habit of just being nice, our "no" loses its power. People-pleasing is probably one of the most dangerous principles we can instill into our children. The terrifying world of cyberspace, with its abundance of child predators, is a reality that we must deal with, especially for parents and those who work with children.

In the educational system, all employees (even IT like myself) are considered mandated reporters where we are expected to be on alert for potential threats that are attempting to take advantage of our children. Along with our own diligence, we need to empower and equip our children with one of their most important weapons—their ability to say no! Teaching them not to speak to or go places with strangers is essential, but it is just as crucial to make sure that our children are comfortable with saying no as early as possible.

As parents, teaching our children can become a serious safety issue as well—those who have suffered abuse themselves often also become abusers. But with our no, we do not have to be a victim. We can have a voice. NO, we do not want to be touched anywhere! NO, I will not touch you there! NO, I do not want to see you there, and NO, you are not supposed to see me there! Let us make sure we are not setting our children up to be vulnerable and unprepared. By teaching children how to say no while they are young, they can prayerfully protect themselves when others might try to take advantage. Beyond that, they will learn not to be nice, life-long sugar coaters. Childhood goes by fast, so we must be proactive.

How many of us have an overly sensitive moral compass that pushes us to go overboard in doing for others when we have never thought of doing anything for ourselves first? When we get on an airplane, we get the same emergency instruction that if something goes wrong with the cabin pressure, before we help anyone else, even our children, we need to put the oxygen mask on ourselves first! The same applies to our lives. We cannot truly give until we have taken care of ourselves first. Even Christ left the people to go away by Himself to pray and talk to God. He knew that without that time and connection with His Father, He would be ineffective in serving everyone else. Real selfishness is only thinking and caring for one's self, but true giving is doing for yourself to be in the best position to help others.

Like with Lauren, our children should not be forced to do anything for anyone else until they've had the opportunity to enjoy the toy or whatever else it may be first. Then we can encourage them to share and to give. For example, for every toy they receive, they might take one toy they no longer use to a homeless shelter and give it to a child who doesn't have one. In my opinion, this is true giving. We have to empower our children with "no" so they can genuinely say "yes"!

It is time for us to develop bully-proof children, who will not fall to pieces when someone calls them outside their name. No more being completely deflated when other insecure children post something negative about them on social media. I believe that once we instill confidence and courage in them, regardless of what the latest trends are, or what they do or do not own, they will know who they are and be excited about their futures.

4. There is always a better, third option

There are a multitude of *great* moments to teach our children how to resolve situations without just outwardly complying. "What are the options here?" is a question that we need to teach our children to ask. We do not need more workers in our technologically advanced world. We need more thinkers and innovators. While earning my Engineering degree in Computer Science from Howard University (Go Bison!), I learned that there is always a better third option that exists, we just have to be willing to search for it. To show kindness in our lives daily, we must be ready to wrestle with this challenge. But, once we do, we can overcome every situation we go through and thus build stronger relationships, more confidence, and clear hearts.

Let's come back to the 'Nice' Family, who have now begun to make the shift to become the new, kinder Baker Family.

Maurice has decided to share with his manager ahead of time that he will no longer be staying late at work to cover any last-minute projects or late requests without prior notice. He has now been better able to focus and is willing to speak up at work to share his ideas to improve performance and efficiency. His ideas have led to a big promotion at work, which in turn gives him more time with his children, Tristan and Lauren.

Because Dad is home more, Lauren is beginning to come out of her shell. She has felt much more comfortable at school now and loves to share with Dad about her day at school and receive his encouragement. Keisha is feeling much better now that Maurice is home more to help with chores around the house. They are now a tag team to help better raise the children and instill confidence in them.

With more time to think and get organized, both a family AND couple vacation are now on the calendar, and Keisha is going back to school for a degree she has wanted for a while. With Keisha's full schedule, Carmen is now allowed to come over only during certain, limited times, with a focus on solutions only!

Tristan is doing much better in his classwork as well as on the baseball team. Following his Dad's example, he has now begun speaking up around his friends about what he will and will not do with them moving forward. Lauren has begun to learn the value of sharing now that she has had the opportunity to play with her toys first. In addition, Mom is more patient and no longer forcing Lauren to share. Mom and Lauren are getting closer, and Lauren is now comfortable to share her thoughts and feelings with her. The word "No" has created a new space where both can gain wisdom and joy by the day.

Limits have begun being built and the Baker Family has turned the corner for the better. With their truths being spoken, they are seeing opportunities that would have never presented themselves in the past. This is a fictional story, but each family and individual who chooses to apply these principles of kindness will see it's fruit. Let's better prepare our children to accomplish their purpose and achieve their goals with a strong and kind foundation at home.

Chapter 11
KINDNESS IN UNCOMFORTABLE SITUATIONS

Life has a way of making us face uncomfortable situations head-on that we would rather continue to brush under the rug. These unaddressed issues affect our health, finances and peace of mind. The question is not whether or not these situations need to be dealt with, but how to treat ourselves kindly through the process.

Fear of confrontation is one of the biggest reasons many of life's challenges (also known as growth opportunities) linger long past the point where it is clear something needs to be done. Whether we realize it or not, we can still be kind and address the truth of a situation without any fluff or hesitancy. We are negatively impacted in the following ways when we deny having these uncomfortable conversations.

> Kindness boldly states it is better to be kind to one person than to live our whole lives being nice.

1. Our attitude changes for the worse

Many of us know the idiom which says, "One bad apple spoils the bunch". The Bible says in 1 Corinthians 15:33, "Do not be deceived: 'Evil company corrupts good habits.'" This is all too true when it comes to being around negative people. It's so funny that in all my years of youth ministry, we focused so much on who the young people hang around, but never mentioned age. Anyone's character, youth or not, can be corrupted by being around the wrong type of people. The inverse of this is also true. If we are around the right people, they will help us find and become better versions of ourselves.

When we are connected to the wrong people in a relationship, whether that's a friendship or closer, our attitude about ourselves will change for the worse. We begin to see ourselves through their eyes, good or bad. When that person feels good about us, we feel good, but when they don't, we don't either. We begin to try to make ourselves look better to them by saying and doing things that we ordinarily wouldn't even think orconsider. This type of codependency can rob us of our confidence, positivity, and self-image.

Dictionary.com lists "attitude" as the manner, disposition, feeling, or position about a person or thing. Our attitude changes when we start making excuses for new people we meet, their bad behavior, and attitudes. We justify their actions as if they can do no wrong. We also get mad when those close to us begin to point out the changes in our character and demeanor they have noticed since we have gotten close with this new person.

2. We are doing things we've never done before

When we are codependent and allow ourselves to be in a negative relationship for too long, we fall into the all too familiar pitfall where we do things we are not comfortable. It is likely that these negative people were already involved in something that you wouldn't ordinarily do, but now that you are with them, you may ever so slowly become open to the idea of it. Just like the idea that it is easier to pull someone down off the table than it is to pull them up, we are yanked down from our values, to a level previously undreamt.

3. Our decision-making process becomes flawed

The effects of staying in bad relationships too long spills over into our decision-making. How we deal with money, what goals and aspirations we have for ourselves begin to degrade, and we are all of a sudden making terrible choices! Our standards become lower, and we lose our sense of importance and shift our short-term decisions to make them happy.

Manipulative partners will often say things like "If you loved me, you would _____". When we lack the confidence to stand up for ourselves, we may comply with a lot of hidden and silent regret. When our attitude, our belief about ourselves, and our decisions begin to change for the worse, we know it is time to end this relationship.

Let's say you do have a conversation to raise your concerns with this person, and you are waiting on pins and needles to see their response. It's important to realize that the majority of us have been conditioned to be nice at all costs, so these experiences are entirely foreign. As a result, we default to common responses to things that we are not comfortable with: we get angry, or we retreat.

The tension is that we think we are personally responsible for other people's feelings when in reality, this is not true. As long as we speak the truth with prayer, love, and compassion when we do communicate, how they respond is entirely up to them! We need to put ourselves in their shoes and do our best to share with them how we would want the same information given to us. Then, we have to be prepared and willing to provide them with space to process what we shared. We cannot be selfish and assume they are relaxed and that things will snap back to normal right away. On both sides, time and space are needed.

I don't believe the old adage that time heals all wounds, but I do think time and physical proximity are personal boundaries that we can implement to give control back to that person or ourselves. Even if this means blocking their phone number, muting their text messages, or unfollowing them on social media. We have to be honest with ourselves and kindly allow both parties the choice to continue or discontinue the relationship.

The Bible says in Matthew 18:15 (AMP), "If your brother sins, go and show him his fault in private; if he listens and pays attention to you, you have won back your brother." Whether or not we believe this, having tough conversations like this strengthens relationships and allows them to go to the next level! The growth and maturity that occur when we acknowledge how our actions affect us will enable us to build tighter bonds with our loved ones. We're often too nice to even think about correcting someone, but I believe that for the peace of our own hearts and the potential closeness that can happen, it is well worth it!

How to End a Bad Relationship

Relationships can lead to many uncomfortable and tense situations. What about knowing exactly when it is time to end a bad relationship? So many times, others can see when it should be done before we do!

Many of us have been there or will eventually have to end a relationship. Relationships are 100% unavoidable in this life, so we all will have our share of bad ones. Some relationships, such as with family members, cannot be chosen. Others, such as friendships, employee/boss, player/coach, and boy/girlfriend, we have more opportunities to choose. A boss can hire who they want, and employees can decide where they best fit. A player can choose a different team to play on, and coaches can recruit different athletes to join their team.

When we realize it is time to leave a job, organization, or relationship, the internal battle begins. Where else would I be able to find a job? Will the other team allow me to play my game? Will anyone else accept me as their boyfriend or girlfriend? We are all human, so our heartstrings often become connected to other people. Sometimes we must learn to separate ourselves from that relationship.

I believe, deep in our hearts, we all know when it is time to end a bad relationship, but many romantic relationships are challenging to separate from because our hearts are invested. When dishonesty, mistreatment, and manipulation rear their ugly heads, we have to make a decision. When enough has been done to mandate a separation of a friendship, an intimate relationship, or sadly even marriage, we have to make a decision.

The challenge comes in the time gap between when logical and emotional choices are acknowledged. How many of us linger in the valley of indecision while rationalizing, what Steven Covey says in *The 7 Habits of Highly Effective People* is "telling ourselves rational lies"? We may make excuses for the other person or even feel that we do not deserve better for ourselves. It's shocking how many of us "nice" people allow ourselves to be taken advantage, mistreated and abused. Now, we also have to make sure we are the type of person who will give the best to the person we are in a relationship with. The Word of God states in Proverbs 18:24 that "A man who has friends must show himself friendly." Let me say it right here, we DO deserve the BEST, especially in relationships! Let's break down some steps to end a terrible relationship kindly.

1. Have confidence in yourself

I believe one of the main reasons we stay in negative and harmful situations longer than we should is that we do not have much confidence in ourselves. Somewhere in our lives, we adopted the belief that we do not deserve to be treated with honesty, respect, and kindness. We began devaluing ourselves, and thus opening ourselves up to all types of adverse situations. In turn, now we make excuses for not wanting better for ourselves.

The only way to make it out of these life- deflating circumstances is to be kind to ourselves and exhibit confidence. Confidence is believing in ourselves. We must allow our beliefs about who we are and what we bring to the table to dictate our decisions, especially regarding relationships. Confidence that, as a child of God, we are completely deserving and worthy of not putting up with anything we are not comfortable with!

I believe the hardest part in maintaining our confidence is being willing to separate ourselves from the negative, controlling, and selfish people in our lives. We must not only believe we deserve better but that God will take care of them as He sees fit! More times than not, our guilt-ridden, negative, internal playlist replays messages in our heads that make us think that even though we are not happy, we feel controlled and manipulated. We feel as though we are actually responsible for others! We have to separate from these individuals and leave them to make the necessary changes in their lives if they no longer want people separating from them.

Though it may not feel like it, this is a kind thing we can do for that person! We can no longer be a spiritual, emotional, mental, or financial crutch for them. They will have to grow on their own. Regardless of what they do, we are NOT responsible for them, their feelings, their negative attitudes, or their choices. We have enough to deal with ourselves!

I distinctly remember, as a teen and young adult, I had no confidence whatsoever. During this time, I honestly believe I had the shortest relationship in middle school history. It lasted for one day—only 24 hours. The struggle was REAL. I was so clueless and mainly terrified to have a girlfriend, and I didn't even know what to do in a relationship anyway. After years of wanting a relationship but never having one, I was hurt significantly.

Even through my insecurity, I knew deep down that it was time to end it. I wanted better! But how to do it was foreign to me, like speaking a new language. I cannot remember what I ended up saying. I know it was definitely clunky, and not clear at all. After we broke up, it strangely felt like nothing changed! We continued to talk every day, like nothing had ever happened. On the confidence meter, I felt as if I was at a negative 20.

My second girlfriend was a short and somewhat less intense relationship, but still not what I wanted at all. She was afraid for us to be seen together at church. I had to park down the hill when I came to see her among other things that did not make me feel awesome about myself. When we did eventually end things, I think both of us knew it wasn't a healthy relationship at all. I can't remember what was said, but I felt better ending this one, knowing that it was for the best. Though I may not be as seasoned in relationships as others, I eventually developed enough confidence to meet, date, and then marry the third girl I have ever dated, and it has been the best 14 years of my life!

If you do not have the level of confidence where you dare to say no, it is time to develop it, beginning today. Learn new skills, exercise consistently, update your wardrobe, or do whatever you feel you need so you can know that, though you are leaving something or someone behind, what is ahead of you will be that much better! This will definitely increase your confidence and, trust me, make you look that much more attractive! Fellas, real women want a man with confidence!

2. Write out the reasons why it is time to leave

A powerful quote from an unknown writer reads, "A pen can write what words can never say." This statement has transformed my view on writing things down and has truly inspired me to make the practice of journal reflection part of my daily life. A lot of us have never taken time to honestly write out our thoughts and feelings to help process where we are. Whether it be physical or digital, this practice of journaling is therapeutic, emotionally cleansing, and surprisingly freeing!

Along with journaling, I believe everyone who desires to be married should have a list of precisely what they are looking for in a future partner. Write down everything you would want in an ideal spouse, down to their features, character, and positive habits—everything you want. Also, add things that you do NOT want to deal with, or what I call deal-breakers.

Once you have written down what you are looking for in a partner and after you have taken the time to get to know the other person past their attractive looks, this list will help you identify the apparent reason why it is time to end the relationship. Life is short, and the time we spend dating and looking for "the one" must be productive!

3. Discuss with a trusted, impartial friend

Once you have your list of what you want in a future spouse, see where the holes are in your current relationship and share these with a close friend. Hopefully, this friend is impartial and wants the best for you. They can see if you're way off in your thinking or making mountains out of molehills in regard to what your mate is doing or not doing. It helps to bounce your list off someone else. Sensitive and personal things like this are best shared so you can hear yourself say them out loud and in person. Your friend can ask clarifying questions to get to the specific root of what it is you desire in the other person. This list, along with your close friend, will help you develop discerning infrared vision to help avoid connecting with those who are not what you want. Your close friend can also help you compare the list of characteristics with the person you're considering.

Your friend can even help you practice what might be an awkward conversation. They can pretend to be your partner as you discuss, based on your list, why it is time to end the relationship. This step can be invaluable, especially when tough conversations are something we avoid at all costs. This safe space will help you work through it and help prevent you from slipping back into an already toxic situation afterward.

Even after breakups, many of us "nice" people sadly allow things to continue as if the relationship never ended. We still take phone calls, do things for them, or go out with them just like before. This is not a healthy way to end a relationship, and our friends can help us deal with the emotional pain separation causes.

I do not believe the "let's just be friends" line when intimate dating or engaged relationships end. I do not believe that men and women, in general, should be friends. To me, they are either associates, brothers, or sisters in the family of God, or potential spouses. Though painful, I believe it will be best, in the long run, to allow our hearts to piece themselves back together to prepare for our future spouse. God didn't create us to date and break up, much less divorce countless times until we find "the one." This creates a tumultuous precedent, especially when we are married, and children are involved. There is a level of kindness we must show ourselves to avoid the detrimental hamster wheel of relationships and broken hearts. Our friends can kindly support us in listening, asking questions, and challenging us so we will be able to move forward.

4. Courageously disconnect from the source of the problem

Fear of rejection is a huge reason why a lot of people do not want to even bother having the tough, breakup conversations. They are afraid that it will potentially or completely fracture their relationship, so they outright deny their real thoughts and feelings. Those fearful of rejection will even argue with friends and family members who have already seen the issues going on in the relationship. Avoiding uncomfortable conversations can again lead to being too nice when you allow yourself to be continually mistreated and taken advantage of in some way. Or you end up inwardly resentful against that person every time you see them.

God showed me a long time ago that spiritual issues do not merely expire. If we do not learn to deal with our negative emotions like rage, sadness, bitterness, or jealousy, they just pile up like trash. Just like when you miss taking out the trash one week, and then it's that much harder the next time because you need to take out both weeks' trash! This is a spiritual issue. We sit on unresolved issues and just let the minutes, hours, days, weeks, months, and years add up. Sadly, our procrastination makes what we have to do exponentially more difficult.

This is not what God wants for us! We are not supposed to make excuses for others mistreating us for any reason. How many of us have heard rationalizations like, "Oh, they're having a bad day, they are not like this all the time." This is a serious statement that should be addressed with a counselor, especially if this and any other situation is happening regularly. Cecil, my wise friend who has been a big brother to me and is also a fellow youth ministry leader, once said that it is better to deal with the 30 seconds of being uncomfortable and have the conversation than to live with regret for a lifetime. No doubt, these conversations are awkward, but we are always glad to make it through each step and to the very end!

5. Move forward

Once you move forward and happen to see your former mate out in public somewhere, a simple "hello" or smile of acknowledgment is more than sufficient if you are comfortable with that at the time. We do not owe them anything! We are not responsible for their feelings whatsoever. There is no need to start a conversation if you know that not enough time has passed for you to be able to see them without feeling hurt, disappointed, or angry. I believe that the emptiness we feel during a breakup (romantic relationship or friendship) is painful, no doubt about it. We have to let that hurt and disappointment breathe and run its course. We need to feel and process these emotions, then we will be in a better place to analyze what went wrong, we can begin improving ourselves, and focus on attracting the kind of people we want to have in our lives.

Part of the process of ending the relationship should involve forgiveness. Forgiveness is an intimate and profoundly spiritual principle. When hurt has occurred in a relationship, it is so easy to hold onto anger, bitterness, and unforgiveness once it is over. We know the reason for ending the relationship, now it is time to empty our hearts of these negative feelings and replace them with positive emotions like forgiveness, joy, and peace.

The process of recovering from an ended relationship is complicated, but it is not meant to be something done regularly. Tragically, most people believe that holding onto unforgiveness actually penalizes or hurts the other person, but this is not the case whatsoever. Part of being kind to ourselves when ending a relationship is to offer and extend forgiveness. This does not mean we have to communicate to them the fact that we are going to forgive them. This is for us to decide in our own hearts when we are ready and mean it.

We have to have the courage to be alone for the necessary timeframe to address our issues of unforgiveness and recover. Part of this recovery is to forgive ourselves for any bad decisions, words, actions, or reactions we have committed during the relationship. Forgiveness is essential for your emotional health moving forward. We should look back and work to understand what occurred in the relationship. Once we've done that, we look ahead and focus on what is to come in our lives. We are not meant to stay stuck in the past!

Moving on from a bad relationship is challenging, no doubt. This life is too short to be unhappy in a relationship that simply is not scratching where it is itching for you. You deserve better for yourself. Be kind to yourself, forgive yourself, seek to improve in the areas in which you know you need improvement, and trust that God has the best in store for you! This will help you make it through!

Chapter 12
KINDNESS TOWARDS SPOUSES AND SIGNIFICANT OTHERS

Let me get straight to it: It is time to transform our marriages! Marriage is the doctorate level of all human relationships. Married couples know how challenging it can be to stay connected with all the busyness of work, exercise, children, school, and now keeping up with social media. If we are not being deliberate in staying close to our spouses, everything else will get in the way. We have to stay focused on our priorities and make space for everything important to us, and our marriage should be one of our top priorities. Let us break down how we can use kindness to advance our marriages and keep striving for improvement.

> Being nice is always lose-win; kindness is always WIN-WIN!

1. Listen intently

The Bible says in James 1:19, "Know this, my beloved brothers: let every person be quick to hear, slow to speak, slow to anger." One of the hardest things to do in a relationship is to deliberately, patiently, and attentively listen to your partner. Leaning in, keeping eye contact, and restating what they said to make sure you understand—all of that can make a significant impact on the connection and intimacy you can have with your mate.

Husbands, how many times have we heard from our wives how we do not listen? It's time to turn that around! Listening is an active verb. The definition is:

> *1. to give attention with the ear; attend closely for the purpose of hearing; give ear.*

> *2. to pay attention; heed; obey (often followed by to).*

The question we need to answer is: what makes it most difficult for us to genuinely listen to our wives? Usually, we face this struggle when we are already tired. We might be tired from a long day at work, of dealing with our boss getting on our case, or maybe leading people who are not motivated to step up to the plate. And then after work, maybe the car is acting up, perhaps we're getting emails from the kids' teachers. The point is, we are stressed! But we husbands already know on our way home that our wives need our ears. She has had her own challenges that day, and, like her husband is expecting of her, she depends on us to be available to her. Not so much to solve the problem for her, but to be that safe space where she can unload her burdens, stresses, and worries on someone who she knows truly loves her and wants the best for her heart.

2. Staying ready > Getting ready

It is always easier to stay in shape as opposed to getting fit. If we wait until we have high blood pressure, are extremely overweight, or have overstressed organs, it will only be more difficult and more costly to get back into top physical condition. The same goes for our marriages. We have to be deliberate and thoughtful ahead of time to ensure that neither person is too tired, hungry, or sleepy to show our spouses that we truly care about them.

In Stephen Covey's book *The 7 Habits of Highly Effective People*, the first habit is to Be Proactive. Simply put, it means to think and prepare for important goals and tasks ahead of time. In a relationship, just like with our health, we have to take preventative measures. We cannot wait until we are faced with a significant problem or an emergency.

How can we be proactive in a marriage? One great way is to learn our spouse's love language. Gary Chapman wrote an instant classic. His book *The Five Love Languages* helps us understand what our spouse likes and doesn't like and how to scratch where it itches for them. This book has helped me transform my own marriage.

My wife and I went through the book together, and we discovered that everyone has a primary and second love language. I learned that my primary love language is physical touch, and my secondary language is words of affirmation. When she fills my Love Tank through her words and affection, I'm more responsive to her, and it helps me work through whatever challenges I'm facing. Antoné's (Toni for short) love languages are acts of service and quality time. I know when I consistently take out the trash, clear the sink of dishes, help fold clothes or straighten up the den, and sit in the same room with her as she studies or works from home, these proactive gestures are filling her tank. In turn, we feel closer, and everything is better for both of us. By taking the time to fill each other's Love Tanks, we show each other true kindness.

Being forward-thinking can transform the anger, bitterness, and frustrations that often leave hearts and emotions in pieces after a war of words. Each of us has to be forward-thinking in seeking new ways to serve our spouse. These little gestures add up to make significant dividends later on! I would suggest that all married couples grab a copy of Chapman's book and read it together.

We can apply these same principles to how we approach conversations. How many times have we avoided speaking up, being too nice, or ended up lying about our real thoughts and feelings about one situation or another? We hold onto our anger and bitterness until these toxic emotions resurface the next time we get upset. It is vital for us to always be forward-thinking, learning how to appropriately speak our truth before it becomes a real issue or and we blow up.

I want to take a moment to remind everyone that we are not responsible for how our spouse feels (or anyone else for that matter)! What we are responsible for is the tone in which we share and speak our truth to them. In being proactive, we communicate early on that we have something to share and set aside a suitable time to talk. We can use the Sandwich method which in this instance means to share a positive affirmation, share the concern and then follow-up with another positive affirmation. While doing this, we can hold our spouse's hand and rub it softly or gently touch their shoulder (husbands, this is GOLD!), and smile while we are sharing. These methods are just to sensitively convey the message along with sincerity, support and love.

Make sure that you include a specific solution you'd like to see happen moving forward. This is an ideal conversation. Most wives will melt and accept whatever you have to share and be willing to make the necessary changes. I believe that as men and husbands, we are built to be the initiators and our wives the responders. But where we most need to initiate is with tough conversations, with much prayer along with viable solutions. We need to work to help our marriages stay on a growth track, never to become stagnant and empty. When we continue to work, our marriages grow stronger and healthier.

3. Do things together

My wife has a personal goal to lose weight (and is well on her way), but she has had her challenges along the way. I was on my own fitness journey, mainly using workout DVDs in our basement, but I was never as consistent as I wanted to be. I was struggling with knee pain after any workout or run that I did, and I didn't see much progress toward where I wanted to be physically. Finally, we went on a cruise with her parents, and we worked out together on the boat each day.

One thing I know about Toni, she thrives when she can do activities along with other people. I finally decided that I had to join her gym and work out with her every day until she got to her fitness goal. That decision was a game-changer for our marriage! At this point, we have consistently gone to 5 a.m. workouts together for several months. We feel so much better. We both sleep restfully, and we eat healthier due to our consistency. We have seen so many other benefits in our lives from the single decision I finally made to work out with my wife.

I believe that whatever we want our spouse to improve or change, we should be willing to do it with them or, at minimum, support them towards achieving. I cannot think of anything more meaningful and helpful than not only talking about the changes you want to see but partnering with them to help both of you win. The fact is husbands, that when our wives win, we win too! By working together toward a specific goal, you both grow in that area and develop a deeper level of intimacy. There is not one negative thing that can come from a spouse *kindly* joining the other to grow and mature in any way!

Say, for instance, you are working on the budget. There is usually one spouse who is better equipped to manage the finances. Without question, in my marriage, that would be my wife. To meet our financial goals and avoid paying the stupid tax (things like timeshares, home water filtration systems, or unplanned school loans...*don't* get me started!), every person, couple, and family must have a specific plan. But one spouse doing this alone is working at a fraction of the real power of a couple. When both husband and wife work together towards winning financially, even if one spouse is not as talented in that area, the results will yield even better results.

Husbands, when we give our support and attention towards understanding what's going on with the bills, it helps us develop a sense of unity that can sometimes be missing in a marriage. A common cause of divorce is financial issues, but I believe this often occurs when things like bank accounts and account logins are kept separate. In my opinion, for a successful marriage, bank accounts should be shared, and both spouses should have equal access so that each can see what's going on at all times if they choose. Being willing to patiently explain and share what's going on helps build a strong foundation, brings spouses together, and enables both to be equipped to pick up the ball in the event should something go wrong. This balance is what winning looks like in any marriage. This one step can transform a marriage that is struggling today.

What I hope more Christian couples would implement consistently is praying together and reading a devotional book that is specifically for couples. Even more than the other activities you can do together, spending intimate time together discussing, sharing, crying, praying, and opening up about various topics are potent aspects of your marriage. These vulnerable activities have the power to break down any previously erected barriers between you and your spouse. There are thousands of fantastic books that have been written to help marriages continue to grow. As with the plant world, our spiritual life is determined by the amount of consistent growth that is occurring. When plants stop growing, they instantly begin dying. We have to be proactive about experiencing growth in our marriages.

The recent devotional book my wife and I read is called, *The One Year Love Language Minute Devotional* by Gary Chapman, and it is POWERFUL! When you carve out and prioritize time with your spouse to bring to the surface real concerns and issues that may be going on in your home, with your children, parents, or friends in the safety and sanctity of your own home, there can be real breakthroughs, healing, and restoration!

In my years of youth ministry, I have seen that in a big group, there is usually one young person's home that becomes the "safe space" where other young people love to hang out. This family has created a welcoming atmosphere in the entire house, and when parents can communicate openly with each other, that ability usually transfers down to their children. Generations X, Y, and Z are searching desperately for authenticity, community, and spirituality (not just religion), and sadly, so many of our homes are void of all of these. Parents, you are your children's first youth pastors! They learn about God from how we interact and how we share with them who God is to us. The church will only confirm and solidify what you've already been instilling. To lead your children closer to God, you have to start in your relationship with your spouse. Both of you bring a level of spirituality that can be exponentially increased as you grow spiritually together, and that can only happen when you each make it a priority to consistently have both personal and couple's devotional time every day.

For those of you who are in long-term relationships, I'd like to pause and strongly encourage you to consider marriage. It's like making it into the major league from the minors! Be kind to that woman, because either you've got a winner or a chicken dinner! Show her, her family, and friends that you are a real man who is ready to dedicate your life to her! Women, if you know that your man is a straight-up jive turkey, it is time to kindly break the relationship off. You are worth being chosen in marriage. Ladies, do not let him off the hook and continually be "available" to him! If he knows he does not have to commit, then time has already shown he will not! I cannot imagine how difficult it would be to end things with a "long-term booty call," but God wants the best for his children. Just ask yourself, is this current situation working out in your favor? If not now, when?

There are so many benefits that come with marriage. Of course, there are a few items you'll want to check off the list before you tie the knot. Definitely, on your way to the league, I would advise going through premarital counseling. A great book to read during the counseling stage is called *Before You Say "I Do"* by H. Norman Wright. Fellas, it is time to LOCK IT UP. It only gets better in marriage, individually and together!

Being Kind to Your Spouse

You might think that kindness is par for the course in every married couple, but we cannot assume that these days. But that does not mean there is no hope. Many couples are not living their best lives. Everybody is dealing with so much on their own and rarely lets their spouse know. When frustration at work, poor health habits, and lack of sleep pile up over time, there are guaranteed to be plenty of arguments and poor decisions in that home. The kind option would be to alert your spouse to what you're struggling with and allow them to assist you in carrying the load or to be more patient with you as you work to resolve it. There has to be a shared game plan and constant communication to win as a couple so that you each can be the best spouse you can be!

I have heard that, in a catastrophe, the leader is the one who is the calmest. I believe that there are different seasons where this role can switch from husband to wife. I am challenging all husbands (including myself) to step into the part of the leader in the home and to clearly and kindly state the goals and direction the family will take. I would strongly encourage husbands to prepare by reading, watching videos, finding and attending seminars with their spouse, and asking other trusted married men what they do to win at home. The goal is to educate ourselves well enough so that when we do communicate, our wives see that we know what we are talking about and that we have done the research necessary to begin putting these new goals in place. What wife would not love to see their husband taking the initiative like this?

Now, I want to speak to the wives for a moment. I know that we, as men, do not always pay as close attention as we should. We miss so many of your wants, desires, likes, and dislikes when you express them verbally to us. This is an area that still requires growth for me. Instead of assuming and asking your husband to try to remember and figure out what you like for gifts, date nights, and trips, I would suggest you kindly give him a list that clearly states what you do and do not like in each of these areas. You can speak to him while you're eating a meal together. This will help your husband remember and focus on what you like and prefer, at least for a season. He can use this fresh reminder of the things you enjoy so that when you are about to go out, or a birthday or anniversary is coming up, he can have a reference list of things he can begin planning accordingly. He does not need to tell you which of the ones you have listed for him he has chosen, and you will be surprised and grateful for the thought he has put into whatever it is.

Overall, please be kind to your husbands. We are more sensitive than we let on, and it truly hurts us to know that we have disappointed and let you down. Sadly yes, we do have a narrow focus at times on our work, bills, and ministries and just need some help to be re-energized and gently reminded of what you like and prefer. You can complain to your girlfriends if you want to, but why not be forward-thinking?

Now husbands, if our wives do help us by clearly stating what they like and prefer, we simply cannot afford to lose or forget this information! It will be worth it to see the smile on her face and the joy in her heart when she opens those gifts or gets to where you are taking her for a special occasion! We will feel like superheroes, and our wives will show their appreciation.

Tone Matters

Many men and husbands either have or will eventually come to the realization that vastly more important than what we say to the women in our lives is our tone and how we share whatever it is. How we speak to our spouse is vital. We must learn to speak kindly to our spouse, especially when we are frustrated or when we are sharing bad news. Of course, there will be situations both inside and outside the home that are disappointing and frustrating, but someone needs to maintain their tone when vital conversations need to be had. When we have something difficult to communicate, it is essential that especially us men do a few things before we have the conversation to share the information kindly.

Before you have that conversation with your spouse…

1. Write out the issue you have with potential solutions

There's a book that completely changed my life and my belief in the power of reflective journaling. In *Write it Down, Make it Happen: Knowing What You Want and Getting It*, Henriette Anne Klauser wrote a chapter on the importance of writing out whatever the situation is, including everything frustrating about it, along with whatever potential solutions you can come up with. There is so much power in putting our muscles to use to express our thoughts and feelings on paper, and writing out thoughts, not even on a laptop or tablet but with an old-school pen and paper. I have used this process for so many issues, and seeing the problem written out gives me an objective look. It helps me to process the situation before I speak, so I am not surprised by my own thoughts.

When you have something extremely frustrating to share with your spouse, taking a few moments to write it out, especially when you are angry, can help you to be kinder to your spouse. It seems impractical, but it's better to avoid significant explosions. Big issues must be discussed, but the question is when.

2. Discuss the issue with an older or wiser married person that you trust

I tell the young people at church all the time, the people they ask for help or advice should have three qualities: They are older and/or wiser than you (though younger individuals can still be wiser at times), they want the best for you, and they do not need anything from you. Married men definitely do not talk with each other enough. So many arguments could be easily avoided if you would talk the situation out with a friend who you know has a healthy and loving relationship with his spouse. He can be a sounding board for you after you have begun to process the situation, and he can also potentially share helpful advice with you.

I thank God for my friends who have become brothers—Mike, Brian, Tawanda, and Thomas. I have known these guys for going on 17 years now. We have our group chat, we hang out and watch the Washington Football Team and Wizards games, we meet up for breakfast at IHOP, we pray with each other, and we tell each other the truth. I do not have any physical brothers, but I consider these guys blood.

We have learned to trust and be there for each other through all sorts of drama. They have helped me avoid overreacting to so many situations that I swore were worse than they actually were, and I am eternally grateful! I pray you have these types of friends in your life. When we talk to the wrong people about challenges at home, we often end up making things even worse than they already were. Most of our spouses love that we have friends of character who we can trust will share wisdom when we do speak with them.

3. Use a gentle touch while speaking with your spouse

We discussed writing out a potential plan for how you will move forward positively and speaking things out with a trusted friend. We also talked multiple times about using the Sandwich Method. Now, let's add physical touch to complete the trifecta.

When we gently hold our spouse's hand, touch their shoulder, or rub their arm or knee while we are speaking with them as considerate and thoughtful husbands, we can melt whatever angst or volatility our spouse may currently have in their heart. Husbands, we can be such ogres to our wives sometimes, especially those of us who have been married for more than five years. I know personally that we can simply get lazy and pull back the effort we gave when we first wanted to get with them while we were dating. This is when true love and kindness need to be reengaged and consistently applied! Especially when either of us is upset or frustrated, we need to use that gentle touch to regain a calm atmosphere.

These three steps, along with much prayer, complete honesty, and transparency with yourself and God, will guarantee a positive conversation with your spouse where you can display kindness to her and at the same time draw closer to her, which is no doubt a win-win!

Finding the Right Person

I believe everyone who desires to be married should have a list of exactly what they are looking for in a future partner. Include their features, character, and positive habits—everything you want. Also, add things that you do NOT want to deal with or what I call deal-breakers. I knew I wanted someone who loved ministering to young people. My spouse would have to understand why I run *towards* the crazy, immature, and unpredictable teens when most run the opposite way! This helped narrow down the possibilities of who I'd want to marry. I challenge you to do the same.

Obviously, most of us know we cannot date every available person of the opposite sex. We must have clear criteria for who we want to be with. We must identify this clearly so we do not end up wasting so much of our and the other person's time and emotional energy, knowing that a relationship with them would not benefit us in any real, meaningful way.

I would like to point out that no one, including ourselves, is perfect, so it might be unrealistic that one person will fulfill every single metric we have listed. But if that person meets 80% of what you have on your list, prayerfully move forward! I have heard this referred to as the 80/20 Rule. Basically, no person on planet earth will meet 100% of what we have on our list, but if we find someone who meets 80% of our list, we have potentially found a winner! By only moving forward with someone who has 80% of what you're looking for, you will save yourself significant time, energy, and stress!

Remember that your deal-breakers are non-negotiable! Keep your standards high and trust that God wants the best person for you. Remember, while you're waiting to find this person, you can take that same time to focus on becoming what you want from your future mate! While we are keeping our eyes open for "the one," we can focus on becoming the one! This process can take time and cause emotional pain, no doubt. I believe that we should not date anyone and not have made a positive impact on their lives, even if the relationship ends. Ideally, we should be the type of person that, even when the relationship ends, our former partners can honestly say that they are glad they dated us!

Why do so many relationships have to end so poorly? Whoever we spend the most time with, with friends and intimate relationships, these people should make our lives better for having spent so much time with them, not worse! We must have standards for who we will associate ourselves with. This is how we can be kind to ourselves because not everyone is worth dating.

It may sound harsh, but many of us have knowingly wasted a ton of time and emotional resources bouncing back and forth from relationship to relationship, like a pair of sneakers in the dryer, wishing we had the time and pieces of our hearts back! Making a list of what you want will help you not only to avoid unnecessary heartache but help you focus your limited time and energy on who you know will make you the most fulfilled.

Chapter 13
NICE GUYS DO FINISH LAST

The struggle of being a nice guy is something I can relate to all too well. Growing up, I was never involved in a fight. Not a real one, anyways. Three close situations come to mind.

One happened when my late cousin Wayne (R.I.P) and I were coming back from hanging out. My Aunt Gretna was a professor on a college campus, so we had access to every type of sport imaginable there. Baseball, basketball, swimming, tennis—you name it, and we did it all. I honestly cannot remember the reason, but that day Wayne and I were arguing, and he was definitely more upset about it than I was. He shoved me pretty hard, and I did not want to fight at all. My yet-to-be-identified peacemaker side came through, and I just kept walking into the apartment. I think the only reason the argument did not continue was that we walked right into another argument going on in the apartment. My uncle was upset with my cousin Eddie about not cleaning up after himself, and it was very tense when we opened the door. That helped diffuse the issue Wayne, and I was having.

> Being nice is conditional, kindness is unconditional.

Kindness Defined

The second time was when I was a freshman in college. I was on my way home from Howard University to our home close to Coolidge High School in N.W. Washington, D.C. It was the middle of the afternoon, so the bus was pretty much empty then. Two drunk guys got on the bus and chose to sit right next to me. I was listening to some Sade (I loved me some Sade), and these two guys kept asking me random questions about who knows what. They started admiring my yellow and gray Sony Walkman tape player with orange buttons (I know, I am old).

One of them was like, "Hey man, let me listen for a little bit." I was like, "Naw, you good, I am about to get off so…" Then, all of a sudden, he grabbed my tape player! I yelled, "Hey man!" and tried to grab it back but did not notice he already had his big left fist up. WHAM! He knocked me right on my top lip. I went numb, and before I knew it, the bus driver came and shoved the drunks off the bus and got back my now broken tape player. I was so salty. But again, I did not want to push things any further, even if I had had the chance.

The last altercation I was in happened when I was playing basketball with my friend Kevin at the old Columbia Union College gym (now Washington Adventist University). We were younger than most of the guys we played with. Kev was not necessarily a fighter, but he did not back down either. Kev made a foul call on one play, and one hyper-aggressive guy we were playing against did not agree with him. He stepped to Kev aggressively, and before I knew it, he swung on my man!

Kev swiftly ducked the punch! I happened to be close enough and stepped towards Kev to have his back. Though I was trying to calm the situation down, the angry dude also wildly swung at me! The only thing I knew to do was to duck the punch as well. After this, Kev and I simply backed up and said we were not there to fight. We grabbed our stuff and just walked out of the gym. The "fight" was over.

Being a nice guy affected me outside of just physical altercations. Throughout my life, I was always afraid to approach pretty girls, and college made things no different. I will never forget, at the end of my freshman year, I met this attractive young lady in one of my engineering classes. Through all the countless hours spent studying and meeting with the professor during office hours, we became close, and we began to hang out. I remember, one night, I asked her if she wanted to go bowling or something with me. She told me, "Yeah, we would like to go." Confused, I was like, "Uh, what do you mean, 'we'?" She responded, "Yeah, if you want to take me out, then my friend gets to come too." As I look back now, being older and wiser, I can appreciate how young women do things to stay safe, but back then, I was so mad!

How could she try to manipulate me by getting me to pay for her *and* her friend to go out? I think this was the first official time I ever said no. I told her I wouldn't be able to take both of them. She was confused. I told her that I wanted to go out, just the two of us, but she didn't budge. I said ok, and we parted ways. That was pretty much the last time we spoke, although she had the nerve to send me a letter that summer with a picture of her in a bathing suit. She was pretty, but I had decided that I simply would not allow any woman to manipulate me like that. Deep down, I realized the Spirit of God wanted me to be more confident, not bending my standards for just a pretty face.

Today, sadly, many men are being exposed for being the complete opposite of nice. Abuse of power, control, manipulation, degrading of women, and many other vices have been brought to the forefront. Some NFL team owners, Hollywood executives, Olympic coaches, college professors, and sadly some pastors have disregarded what true manhood represents. Real men use their influence to support, uplift and empower others, never to take advantage of anyone, especially women. Our world is in desperate need of godly, spiritual men (and women, btw) with integrity who can face trial and temptation head-on with courage and determination. To do as Ellen White powerfully exclaimed, "stand for the right, though the heavens fall!"

On the opposite end of that spectrum, being too nice has its own set of issues. Typically, we nice guys are silent about what is actually bothering or frustrating us. We rationalize—tell ourselves rational lies—about anything that would rock the boat. Most of us have never even thought about or considered learning any type of conflict resolution. It is exhausting for us to continually say yes to people's requests and expectations of us, but we are paralyzed to even consider saying the word no.

Being too nice isn't just a problem for guys. Nice girls have their own struggles too. They are often culturally raised to keep their parents happy, especially their mothers, so they do not speak up for themselves at any cost. Where they work, live, who they date or marry, and how they spend their money are all determined by their parents. Unfortunately, parents who control their daughters' lives to this degree just set them up to end up with a jive turkey. A jive turkey is a man who has no goals or aspirations. They leech off everyone else, especially their girlfriends, never putting forth any real effort to be responsible for themself. They usually end up living the same year of their lives multiple times in an unending cycle. Controlling a nice girl to this extent will obliterate her freedom, confidence, and guidance to choose a winner with real goals, aspirations, and desires.

I want to touch on five reasons why nice guys (and girls) finish last and how to address them:

1. We become a shell of ourselves

When we are nice, we allow ourselves to be phony and empty on the inside. We have no depth of soul, no convictions, and no firm lines that we are unwilling to cross. There is no way anyone can ever be happy living this way. Nice guys are professional sugar coaters. We build these skills over time, learning how to say just enough to keep our jobs but never advance and grow. And we often end up doing more than we are responsible for because we do not want to be the ones to call someone out for their irresponsibility.

Men need a real identity, and being nice will only give us a shallow existence. Living a shallow life breeds frustration and lack of fulfillment and makes us that much more vulnerable to the enemy's attacks through self-doubt, depression, anxiety, and lack of confidence.

I will never forget the spring semester of my freshman year at Howard University. I was taking courses to officially get into the Computer Science Engineering program, and I was surprised that I was actually doing well in calculus. I was studying every single day for this class and absolutely understanding it (one of the best feelings in the world). I was going to office hours with my professor, spending at least an hour in the stacks daily, I was in a flow. As I was studying one day, the thought came to me, *Man, I am doing exceptionally well in this class. What other areas of my life should I improve on?* At that time, I was involved in church. I was not paying much attention during Bible studies or sermons, but I was delighted about opportunities to feed the homeless. I knew in my heart that I was not pushing myself in all aspects of my life.

As I was pondering all this, an audible, distinct voice spoke to me, saying, "Osei, you are a phony!" The voice was so clear that I stood up in the middle of the cubicles to see who had said it. I looked around and saw other students busy studying, but no one looked like they were actually speaking to me. So, I sat back down, saying to myself, *"That was weird; I wonder where...."* Then the voice came back and said, "Osei, you are a phony! You do not know who you are or what you believe." I came to the realization that it was God Himself speaking to me, and I said, "God, you are right!" That was the end of that conversation, but it was all I needed.

From that day, I was determined to figure out exactly why I called myself a Christian. I was online all summer long while working in the computer science lab. Even though not much work was going on,

I was on a mission. I emailed pastors from other denominations, asking questions on key Bible topics. That was a great time for me! If God had not gotten my attention, I would have continued just going through the motions. I would still only be doing what I was raised to do, not because I was convinced it was correct, but just going along with the flow as a nice guy.

2. Nice guys are not attractive to the opposite sex

In terms of relationships, human nature drives both men and women to desire a challenge. We often believe it's only men who want to hunt, but women want someone with who they can throw ideas, challenges, and controversy and not have them be quickly agreed with just because their partner is afraid of conflict. Some women are more aggressive, but eventually, they will grow frustrated with a nice guy because they are not being strengthened and motivated to do better.

Women simply do not find nice guys attractive. They want a man who can handle his business. They want a man who will not just crumble and be pushed around when life throws curve balls. They want men who stand up when someone tries to take advantage of them. A man who always runs home to momma for help, money, or reassurance will not work for women who are actually going somewhere. Will they grow up and figure out a plan to get things done? Women seek a sense of security from their men. They are attracted to a man with an engaging personality.

Nice guys tend not to disagree, challenge, or question anything. Many women throw thoughts, ideas, and subjects at men to see what they will say. I've noticed that a lot of women will ask thoughtful questions to reveal their partner's character. Nice guys will find some way to cower in their responses, leaving women wondering where the guy's backbone is, no way they see themselves doing anything long-term with this type of guy. Worst case, women with a weak character will take advantage of the nice guy. They might get the guy to pay their bills or be a warm body while it is convenient.

Come on, fellas, do not let that be you! Fellas, there is a place in relationships called the Friend Zone. The Friend Zone is where you are close enough to spend time with them and MONEY on them, but do not receive the boyfriend title. Other versions of this "Friend Zone" are where some women will even allow men to pay their bills, allow for sexual activity, but will never claim you as a boyfriend. Ladies, I know that men also do this as well! Either way, we should all first be kind to ourselves and set our personal boundaries because if someone attempts to place us in the friendzone by these tactics, who's fault is it really? The nice guy or girl that let it happen, or the Jive turkey that attempted and successfully used us?

There is an abundance of information that helps us understand how men and women are wired. I do not believe that men should have many women friends, but I know that some women have a lot of male friends. At times that hints towards an issue that they cannot build healthy friendships with other women. Regardless, the fact is that physiologically speaking, both men and women have sexual desires.

I learned an incredibly powerful principle regarding men and women at a seminar called "Binding the Wounds." The key thing to understand is that when a man receives from a woman emotionally, his body then desires some sort of a sexual payoff. When a man listens to intimate things from a woman, such as her hopes, fears, and desires, these feelings are produced naturally. Let me be clear; it doesn't matter what our bodies do or say as men. A woman always has a right to say no to unwanted or no longer wanted sexual contact. Men must accept her desire or lack of desire and stop said contact with her, no matter how "unfair" it may seem at the time. I believe that once women hear and understand the effect this intimate exchange produces, they will not want to place men in this position. Instead, women should look for great female friends who will not want anything sexual from them and who can receive these emotional aspects and provide support and encouragement.

Men, this is why we cannot have female friends. The Friend Zone space is not for men. Women will want to talk and share intimate things with you to gain a feeling of security. But, more than likely, they are not in a place to give you what you will eventually want sexually. This is again why women should have close female friends while waiting for the safety and security built into a marriage where they can be completely free to share with their husbands all the intimate details of their hearts and be able to share their love with him sexually as well.

Honestly, some women take advantage of men to fulfill their emotional needs and get a self-esteem boost from having a close male friend but do not take into account these truths about men. It is not his fault if you have countless issues with other women, so don't drag him down and put him into an uncomfortable position. Do I believe that men and women can be close? Yes. But I see it more as a brother and sister type of situation, where advice can be given, help can be procured (like on moving day, with a flat tire, or with a different perspective) but nothing more!

Men, do not play yourself and think you will just be her friend, gain her trust, listen to her deep emotional thoughts, and believe that you will not want to become physical with her. This is dangerous, even for the kindest man on earth. Encourage her to pray and search for a great female friend so you won't have to be pent up with these unnecessary desires. I realize this might be an unpopular stance, but I believe proceeding with caution will reduce the frustration of men and the wishful thinking of women.

3. Nice guys are not great communicators

Great leaders have to be excellent communicators. Nice guys usually aren't willing or capable of having the necessary tough conversations with those they lead. There needs to be a balance of what to say and how to say it so that whoever we are communicating with can understand the seriousness of the situation but also hear our compassion towards them. Being afraid of how someone will respond is an unfortunate reason not to have a conversation, especially when it hinders our progress.

It could be a result of being spoken to harshly by others who have more dominant personalities. We hold onto the feelings of being humiliated and demeaned, and we now go to the opposite extreme by refusing to even slightly raise our voices, much less confront others. Most people appreciate hearing the truth directly, with no added fluff or unnecessary pleasantries. They may not like what they hear, but at least they cannot say you did not state the facts clearly.

For example, let's talk about when there is an employee who is not being responsible for what is required of them. They are always late, never where they are supposed to be and have a negative, combative attitude when corrected or challenged. It is probably time to have courageous conversations with them about ending their time there. This also can apply to dating relationships. At some point, we come to realize that the relationship is over. Genuine kindness knows what to do and that the sooner the relationship ends, the better. True kindness provides more time to disconnect emotionally, heal, and move on. Yet, sadly and selfishly, we sometimes keep people hanging on because we like the attention and having the relationship box checked. Yes, the words may come out unclear, and that is why it is vital to keep these types of conversations short.

We do not owe anyone a full explanation for the decisions we make! We share what we feel comfortable sharing, that's all. We are responsible for giving nothing more! This is not being cruel or mean. If we think about it, what will be the benefit of fully sharing why the relationship is over? Will they change? Will they understand and be perfectly fine with our decision? Probably not, but that is ok.

There are a lot of myths that have become law in regard to how we are to end a relationship. So many of us are afraid of that person's anger, and we are not really clear as to why we want to end the relationship. So we stay in the relationship, harboring bitterness and resentment. As I have learned from the book *Boundaries* by Dr. Henry Cloud, if that person blows up at you for ending the relationship, they have a character problem. *They* are the ones with the problem, not you. It is pride that demands a reason why more times than not. If they truly cared for you, they would respect your space and allow you to end the relationship. Love always gives a choice.

The challenge in ending relationships is that we wait until we are ready to end it before we clearly express our frustrations and issues with them. We do not need to apologize for our decision either! No more "'I'm sorry, but...'" because you are NOT SORRY for ending a terrible relationship! This will take a lot of courage, and a strong, supportive group of friends will help make the breakup easier to handle.

4. Being nice makes us tell white lies

When we are solely focused on being nice, we will inevitably find ourselves telling white lies. Dictionary.com defines a white lie as "a minor, polite, or harmless lie; fib." Most of the time, we don't use white lies maliciously. We use white lies to avoid hurting someone's feelings or to avoid trouble. This is dangerous ground to tread. We do not learn or mature from telling white lies. The focus should be on how and when to speak the truth in love, especially in awkward and uncomfortable conversations. But before we can avoid telling white lies to others, we must never tell them to ourselves!

The white lie, "I am fine," when inside you are furious or devastated, is not healthy and can lead to a bevy of misunderstandings and further frustration. We have our cultural pleasantries like, "How are you doing?" But, if we are brutally honest, would we stop and make time to hear them out if that person responds, "I am having a horrible day"? We must be clear and kind, even in how we greet each other!

We are not genuinely asking about others with an authentic desire to hear their responses. We must stop asking questions like this just to be nice! It is time for us to mature and be willing to have tough conversations with kindness as our mode of operation. To stop telling white lies, we have to start assessing our relationships to see why we feel like we cannot tell the truth or accept it. Also, we must improve our communication skills so that we can speak the truth calmly, compassionately, and clearly. Lastly, we must be willing to *receive* the truth from others.

We need to get better at listening kindly. I won't spend too much time here, but if I hear another Christian say" If it is God's will," as a response to another person's sorrow or pain, I'm going to scream! This is not only unbiblical but also trite and downright abusive! We need to allow others to be hurt, disappointed, stressed, sad, or whatever emotion they are feeling without trying to make them feel better with our shallow, empty responses because we are uncomfortable! This infuriates me, and trust me, the people we say it to are done with it! JUST SHUT UP AND BE THERE!

Solomon, one of the wisest people who ever lived, said to "Weep with those who weep," and we should heed this counsel immediately. We're not being Christlike with the blanket statements that make ourselves feel spiritual and like we've helped others. Being physically present, listening empathetically, and being ok in that sad space is how we show kindness during grief. Through encouragement, prayer, and listening, we can avoid telling white lies. We are to be part of allowing the truth to grow, learn, and mature to where God desires.

5. Being nice makes us lazy

I am, at times, probably one of the laziest men I know! I am all about convenience. I like things to be as easy, as close, and as light as possible. I have learned that the smartest people are sometimes the laziest because we'll find the most efficient way to accomplish a goal with the least amount of effort on our part! Being lazy can be tolerable sometimes, but when we start making excuses and rationalizing our behavior instead of putting in the work to improve, we become weak. We lose integrity, and we fail to accomplish our goals. Let's discuss how this happens in our world.

Successful people are not nice to themselves. Instead, they are kind. It is essential to understand that being kind to ourselves involves acknowledging the truth about ourselves. We have to forgive ourselves for past mistakes, treat our bodies well, and actually push ourselves towards God's best in our lives!

Many of us have never pushed ourselves to an exhaustive state for anything. Part of why I love coaching and sports is that I get to help push a group of individuals past what they initially thought they could do, show them how to work together as a team, and teach them how to handle disappointment. So many of us have amazing talents, gifts, and abilities, but we rarely see the results we should be getting. We are missing out in our lives, in our marriages, and in our careers. We're being too nice to ourselves! We need to burst our safe and comfortable bubbles and expose the lies we have told ourselves. Inky Johnson, a powerful motivational speaker, says the "comfort zone is a beautiful place, but nothing grows there." When I first heard this, it hurt, but I knew in my heart it was true. Growth usually means being uncomfortable, but growth is always worth it. We have to lean into being uncomfortable!

I believe that God wants us to be successful! He wants us all to be in positions of influence where we can help more people, inspire others, and cause people to ask us the reason behind our success. Some of us may feel like because we are not the boss, we cannot make any real impact on the overall direction of our job or company. There are countless examples of people who, though not in charge, were able to significantly influence the culture and the direction of their environment in positive ways! People like Mother Teresa, Rosa Parks, and Gandhi, just to name a few, were able to literally change the world through their character, compassion, and focus.

I believe we must use kindness in all our interactions with others so we can be a positive change in the atmosphere of the organizations we are part of. Then we can point to our Lord and Savior Jesus Christ and explain how, by following Him, they can also be successful!

Jesus spoke to everyone kindly, but sometimes He had to move some furniture around (for context read Matthew 21:12-13)! Sometimes we need someone to raise their voices at us to wake us up out of our physical, emotional, or spiritual slumber and into action. We have listened to enough sermons, prayed enough prayers, and now it is time to take our lives to the next level using the power of kindness to push us to the greatness God has ordained for each of us to be!

Chapter 14
COMMUNICATING DISPLEASURE

Okay, someone is doing something we do not like. Because we live on planet Earth, this is unavoidable. But what do we do? Many of us are so "nice," we would never even consider bringing up what we do not like or prefer to anyone. We need to understand how to address when people annoy us, do something we do not like, or put us in harm's way. We should understand ahead of time when to do what. So many times, we introverts will opt for the ostrich method where we stick our heads in the sand and simply pretend something does not bother us when it truly does. This is a perfect example of us being too nice! We can and should address these issues, and we can do so without being a jerk or going entirely outside of our personality.

> Being kind means speaking our uncomfortable truth to others, appropriately, timely, and clearly.

Know the 'Rules'

First, we need to understand the situation. Is this something you can even address with the person? For example, when someone cuts you off on the road, it is a bad idea to follow them and spitefully try to cut them off yourself. Just like I would tell my team when I was coaching basketball, the referees more than not notice when you respond, and not the initial foul. There are clear reasons why we have to know the rules of whatever space or environment we are in, whether it's on the road or a basketball game.

First, we could be the one who is entirely in the wrong. Maybe they did have the right to merge, and you weren't paying attention to the signage. We can be frustrated about something and actually be the one who is causing the problem itself. We can take ten seconds to do a quick search to find out if what we are upset about is indeed something that should not be happening. You can speak with someone from Human Resources, look up your Homeowner Association's rules on loud music, or anything else. You should first do your due diligence and confirm you are right in this situation.

There is usually a built-in method to address a driving or HOA situation. In interactions with people, strangers, associates, friends, and intimate partners, it's not always as clear. When people do or say something that makes us feel uncomfortable, we have to be honest, understanding, and forgiving. This will require a level of patience, understanding, and honesty that many of us are not at currently. When we reach that level, we will be able to strategically navigate from forgiveness to understanding to honesty. We will know what to let go of immediately, what to give understanding toward, and when it is time to speak up and be honest. Kindness will help us to navigate through these situations with joy instead of being quietly bitter and frustrated.

Don't Procrastinate

Clearly address the challenge when it first occurs. We can't live in what author Steven Covey calls an "email haven," where we sit behind a keyboard and try to address a situation indirectly. This can be very passive-aggressive if we have to see and deal with a person regularly.

It is vital to our life's peace that we learn how to adequately address challenges that we face in person when they first occur, if at all possible. Peaceful conflict resolution is a life skill that will open doors that otherwise would remain closed.

When we get ready to approach the person we disagree with, we must remain calm. We cannot think clearly when we're emotional or angry, and our actions will not lead to any peace. When we talk to them, we should have all the relevant details ready to share. Along with using the Sandwich Method referenced in previous chapters, we should have the most recent, accurate, and relevant details of what we are upset about. Ideally, this conversation happens in short order, not too many days or weeks past the initial incident. This way, the person cannot deny what happened, and a constructive solution can be discussed.

It is beneficial that we also have a potential peaceful resolution for what occurred, prepped, and ready to go. More than likely, the other person involved in the issue being addressed doesn't have a working solution in mind, so it can be proactive to suggest what you would like to happen or provide some options. Kindness requires consideration, so these suggestions should aim for a win-win solution.

I believe that there are certain situations that we cannot do anything about (at least without getting ourselves in trouble with the law), maybe because the chances that we see those same people again are minor. Besides honking and yelling at that driver who cuts us off when they can't hear us, there is nothing more we can do about it.

Now, of course, when we have to defend ourselves from physical harm, we should protect ourselves. I do not believe when Jesus told us to turn the other cheek that He meant to allow people to assault and hurt us physically. I do not believe that we are called to allow others to ever mistreat, manipulate, or take advantage of us. We should stand up for ourselves and kindly demand that others treat us the way we deserve to be treated.

Find an Alternative

Sometimes you might have to avoid the annoyances. Especially in work environments, finding ways to not be affected by your coworkers' habits might be the only solution to your situation. Let's say you are sharing a work area and your coworker is playing their music louder than you are comfortable with. You have a hard time focusing, and it is not your musical preference. You can ask them directly to use headphones or lower the volume. Maybe your coworker, for whatever reason, always seems to forget this conversation and continues with the loud music. An alternative could be to invest in some noise-canceling headphones that you can use while working to help you stay focused. This way, you can avoid having to speak with your boss about your concern and continue working in the same space together. This might be the better option and may prove to be the kindest move.

Let it Go

Usually, once we learn to confront the situation with kindness, we can find a viable plan to move forward peacefully. But in the rare instances where no win-win scenario seems to work, we may need to move on. We must choose to let it go because, as Romans 12:18 says, we are called "if it is possible, as much as depends on you, live peaceably with all men." Once we have done our part, we have to move forward.

Once we have the mindset and the attitude of quickly addressing issues, we not only have more peace, but we model for others how to properly resolve issues.

Chapter 15

A CHANNEL OF BLESSING

Ellen White, an inspired writer, wrote on page 77 of *Steps to Christ*, "like the streams of water bursting from a living spring, blessings flow out from Him to all His creatures. And wherever the life of God is in the hearts of men, it will flow out to others in love and blessing."

When we have God's love in our hearts in a consistent, growing relationship, it will motivate us to hunt down opportunities to be kind to others. God is the infinite source of life, love, and blessings. Once we acknowledge Him as such, confess our sins and choose to receive the gifts that He wants so badly to give us, then we can be a channel of blessings.

> It won't be our successes that point people toward Jesus; it will be our kindness.

A channel is a route through which anything passes or progresses. Just like macaroni pasta, pipes, or hoses, channels are made to allow liquids, ink, medicine, and other materials through. But what happens when a channel is blocked or damaged? It can no longer be used to transport substances. Many of us flat out refuse to allow ourselves to be used by God to be a blessing to others. Our western culture has taught us from birth to only look out for ourselves and do whatever it takes to

Kindness Defined

succeed, regardless of others. We damage ourselves tremendously with this behavior. We become clogged channels, or better yet, we end up like the Dead Sea.

The Dead Sea, or the Sea of Salt, is smack dab between Jordan, Israel, and Palestine and is the deepest hypersaline lake in the world. It is called the "Dead" Sea because no plants, animals, or fish can live in it. It has no outlet streams and only receives water. Nothing can grow in it, eliminating most of its usefulness as a body of water. So many of us are incredibly blessed by God, but we are spiritually dead on the inside. We have no joy, peace, patience, or kindness because, for us to have those things, we must be willing channels of blessings.

God wants so desperately to heal us of our hurt, to fix us when we are broken by life, and to remove all the pain from our hearts. God and His Holy Spirit can remove the painful emotions associated with our memories and give us true freedom. That freedom will enable us to acknowledge that yes, we have been abused, attacked, molested, traumatized, and victimized, but we are now FREE! Those bad experiences are no longer controlling us, and they no longer motivate our decisions. Instead, we can choose to be used by God to bless others and share our testimony. Then we can be a channel of blessing and restoration that God can use to help countless others.

Jesus went to the cross and died for our sins so that we could be used by Him. Not in a controlling way, but as a willing participant to bless others. And while we are blessing others, we are being blessed. God wants to give us everything our hearts desire (1 Corinthians 2:9), as long as we are willing to let Him use us to serve, encourage and minister and be kind to those He misses the most! What would our lives look like if we choose today to be a channel of blessing to others through kindness?

I pray that this book has truly transformed your life, as it has for me. I am a living witness to God's delivering power in my own life! It is so exciting to share this journey with you and hear your testimonies of when you trust God and apply the principles of kindness to your life. God wants to bless you more than you want to be blessed, and the greatest joy you'll ever find in life is being a channel of blessing, so God can use you to show His incredible kindness to those He places in your path.

I pray that each of you who reads this wins corporately, financially, physically, mentally, and spiritually. I promise you that if you give Jesus a chance and connect with Him daily, you'll be changed, and others will see something different in you that is inspiring! Let's step into the transformational power of kindness for ourselves, our loved ones, and those with who we interact throughout our lives.

May God's highest blessings be upon you and your families as we choose to be kind and not nice!

Author Bio

Pastor Osei ('Ah-Say') Daniels was born and raised in Washington DC. He attended Takoma Academy for High School and thereafter the prestigious Howard University (GO BISON!). He graduated with an Engineering degree in Systems and Computer Science and is now studying for his Master's in Pastoral Counseling with an emphasis on Life Coaching at Liberty University.

Pastor Daniels has worked with youth for the last 23 years in various capacities such as Youth Elder, Youth Director and Children's and Youth Pastor of the Takoma Park Seventh Day Adventist Church and now serves as one of the Winning Circle Men's Ministry Coaches, led by Dr. Myron Edmonds.

Growing up, he was greatly influenced by his youth leaders, community service leaders, and pastors that helped to encourage and guide him. Pastor Daniels experiences as a youth fostered the desire for him to help today's youth in the same manner. He loves playing and watching basketball, swimming, staying in shape, reading, blogging/writing, technology, gadgets, and traveling. His spiritual gifts are exhortation and teaching. He is the author of, 'Kindness Defined', (First offering in the WINNING DEFINED series) where we will learn how to be KIND and not nice, to say NO with a smile, and to experience the life changing power of kindness in our lives today!

Author Bio

Pastor Daniels and his wonderful wife, Antoné ('An-to-nay' or Toni) have been married for 14 years and they LOVE serving together and aid the needs of all people. His passions are small groups, character development, helping build the bridge between mental health and the church, equipping God's people in their spiritual gifts and showing them the joy and satisfaction in being used to serve others!

Instagram - @kindnessdefined
Facebook - www.facebook.com/KindnessDefines
Website - www.kindnessdefined.com

www.ingramcontent.com/pod-product-compliance
Lightning Source LLC
Chambersburg PA
CBHW050323120526
44592CB00014B/2026